KAYAKING & ADVANCED CANOEING

KAYAKING & *ADVANCED*
CANOEING

A PRACTICAL GUIDE TO PADDLING ON WHITE WATER, OPEN WATER AND THE SEA

BILL MATTOS

Consultant Andy Middleton

southwater

This edition is published by Southwater

Southwater is an imprint of Anness Publishing Ltd
Hermes House, 88–89 Blackfriars Road, London SE1 8HA
tel. 020 7401 2077; fax 020 7633 9499
www.southwaterbooks.com; info@anness.com

© Anness Publishing Ltd 2004

UK agent: The Manning Partnership Ltd
6 The Old Dairy, Melcombe Road, Bath BA2 3LR
tel. 01225 478444; fax 01225 478440; sales@manning-partnership.co.uk

UK distributor: Grantham Book Services Ltd
Isaac Newton Way, Alma Park Industrial Estate, Grantham, Lincs NG31 9SD
tel. 01476 541080; fax 01476 541061; orders@gbs.tbs-ltd.co.uk

North American agent/distributor: National Book Network
4501 Forbes Boulevard, Suite 200, Lanham, MD 20706
tel. 301 459 3366; fax 301 429 5746; www.nbnbooks.com

Australian agent/distributor: Pan Macmillan Australia
Level 18, St Martins Tower, 31 Market St, Sydney, NSW 2000
tel. 1300 135 113; fax 1300 135 103; customer.service@macmillan.com.au

New Zealand agent/distributor: David Bateman Ltd
30 Tarndale Grove, Off Bush Road, Albany, Auckland
tel. (09) 415 7664; fax (09) 415 8892

A CIP catalogue record for this book is available from the British Library.
Publisher: Joanna Lorenz
Senior Editor: Sarah Ainley
Editor: Elizabeth Woodland
Production Controller: Darren Price
Text Editors: Richard Rosenfeld and Paul Grogan
Photographer: Helen Metcalfe
Designer: Nigel Partridge
Jacket Designer: Balley Design Associates
Illustrator: J. B. Illustrations
Indexer: Helen Snaith

Previously published as part of a larger volume, *The Practical Guide to Kayaking and Canoeing*

1 3 5 7 9 10 8 6 4 2

DISCLAIMER
The author and publishers wish to stress that they strongly advise the use of a helmet and flotation aid in all paddling situations. There is no legal requirement to wear either, but paddling is all about taking responsibility for your own decisions, actions and personal safety.

PICTURE CREDITS
All photography by Helen Metcalfe except for the following.
t = top; b = bottom; c = centre; l = left; r = right
Action Images 103t, 104b, 105t, 105b, 114b, 115b. Rob Feloy 61t, 77tr, 96tr, 97t, 97b. Rodney Forte 26t, 28t, 28cr, 28br, 29ct, 68bl, 69bl, 70bl, 70br, 71br. Dino Heald 47b, 112t, 113b. Mark Potts 15b, 17t, 17b, 18bl, 19t, 19b, 33t, 33b, 35bl, 39t, 46br, 47t, 83tc, 83tr, 83b, 109t, 110t. Jason Smith 6t, 7t, 7b, 86t, 86b, 87t, 87b, 90tl, 90br, 91tl. Max Spielman 98, 99t, 99b. Jono Stevens 120t, 120bl, 121t, 121b. Martin Tapely 82, 85b, 109b, 112b, 113t. Dan Trotter 96 (sequence), 123b.

CONTENTS

If you were to ask me, "Mr Nealy, I'm an expert. Should I paddle flooded rivers?" I would say, "No. But if you do, you should read this and learn from my mistakes."
William Nealy,
Kayak (1986)

You must dominate the boat while submitting to the river. You must tune to the shape of the river while persistently focusing the boat's energy. Tough moves require unbending intent.
Jim Snyder,
Squirtboating (2001)

The features you need to check out from a "How do I get out of that?" point of view are the same ones you need to understand in order to make the most of the hole's freestyle potential.
To quote a jet fighter test pilot: "Never put your body where your mind hasn't been first".
Franco Ferrero, British Canoe Union coach,
White Water Safety & Rescue (2000)

"There is nothing — absolutely nothing —
half so much worth doing as simply
messing about in boats." That's what
Ratty said to Mole in Kenneth Grahame's
beloved 1908 novel, *The Wind in the
Willows*. "In or out of 'em, it doesn't
matter. Nothing seems really
to matter, that's the charm of it",
Ratty continued.

Open canoeing is everything
from a chilled-out day on the
lake, through hammering down
a raging torrent, to throwing
some ends in a hole... Open
boating never fails to satisfy.
James Weir, 2001 European
OC1 Freestyle Champion

Introduction

Few outdoor activities can boast the range and scope that advanced canoeing and kayaking do. There are so many different styles of adventurous paddling, and different environments to consider, from steep whitewater rivers to open ocean crossings, dangerous extreme paddling to playboating, and the subsurface gymnastics of the squirt boat to the speed and grace of a sailing canoe. This book is intended to provide some tips and techniques to those who choose to move on from placid water paddling to something a bit more demanding, both physically and mentally. It also gives an overview of the most popular specialist disciplines should you choose to take things even further.

Adventurous Paddling

Before attempting any of the paddling featured in this book, you should be competent at paddling your chosen craft on flat water, and familiar with all the basic paddling and steering strokes. You should be physically fit, able to swim at least 50m vigorously, and capable of remaining afloat indefinitely in your buoyancy aid and other paddling gear. You should also be aware of the limits of your body and how to look after it. Paddling can be hard on you physically and preparation such as warming up and stretching before, and warming down and stretching after can save you from injury or time off the water.

Two sea kayakers enjoying bright sunshine and calm seas – the perfect conditions for a day on the water.

A group of kayakers and canoeists prepare to get afloat at a launching spot on a white water river.

How to Use This Book

Having said all of that, the big difference between placid recreational paddling and the more adventurous ideas in this book is actually in the mind. Beginners sit on or in their boats and paddle around, and very pleasant it is, too. More adventurous paddlers tend to outfit the boat until they are wearing it like a pair of trousers. With experience you will become part of the boat as soon as you get in it – no longer a human attached to a craft, but changed into something else altogether; a kind of centaur with the upper body of a human, and a hard but streamlined lower body. Whether you paddle rivers or in the sea, this kind of thinking is very important, because dynamic paddling means reacting to the forces that act on the boat and the paddle. These are your only points of contact with the outside world. When you drive a car or ride a bicycle, most of your information comes from what you see and hear. You are not truly part of the machine. In a canoe or kayak, you will come to feel. When something

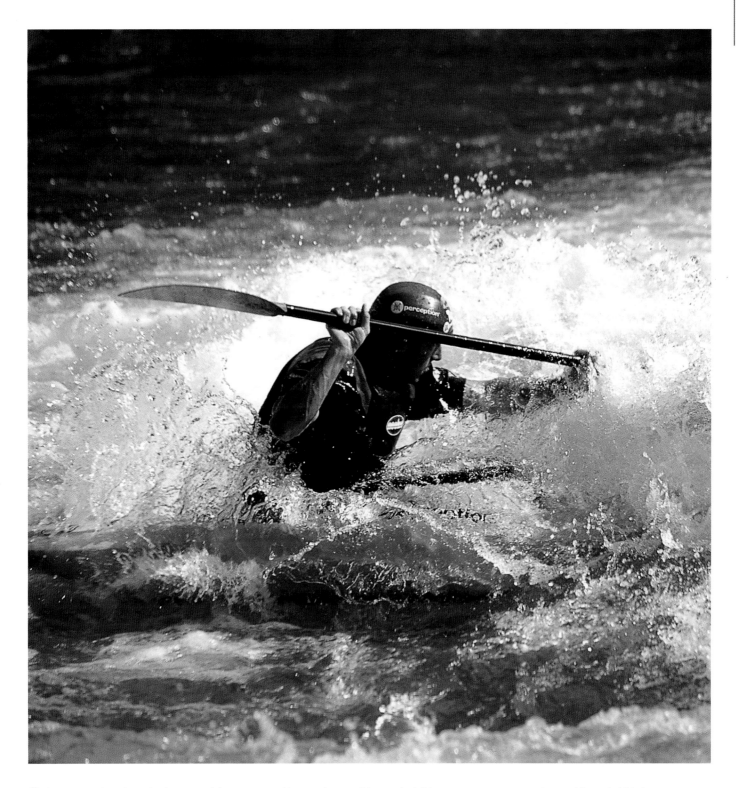

⬭ *An expert kayaker playing on white water. He is paddling a freestyle kayak, designed especially for surfing waves on white water.*

moves the boat or touches its outer skin, you won't just see it happen – you'll feel it just as if something had touched your everyday skin.

So this book is not so much about how to paddle your boat but is intended to provide you with knowledge that will enable you to consider undertaking more adventurous paddling, whether it is in a canoe or in a kayak, in salt water or fresh, in fair weather or foul! The emphasis is on helping you make decisions responsibly and safely. Different sections of the book look at whitewater and open water paddling, and at the different disciplines in which kayakers and canoeists specialize. There is also an introduction to the various forms of competitive paddle sport in which the progressive paddler might take an interest. Finally, and crucially, there is detailed information on key safety and first aid issues that the modern paddler needs to know about.

Don't let the theory put you off. There is nothing like water-time as long as you approach it sensibly and safely, so if there is paddling to be done, go and do it, and use this book as a reference to make sense of what you've learned for yourself.

ON MOVING WATER

WHITE WATER PADDLING

Kayakers and canoeists with an adventurous streak gravitate towards white water paddling. The plastic revolution and the subsequent trend towards short boats have made the turbulent waters of steep rivers and creeks accessible to more people, and spawned the explosion of white water sport that emerged in the late twentieth century.

But what is white water, sometimes described as wild water? The terms describe any water, usually in a river, that has rapids with fast flowing sections where the shape of the river bed causes waves and currents that are chaotic and unpredictable. When the turbulence is pronounced, the water becomes aerated, as if air is being vigorously beaten into the water, creating its white and bubbly appearance.

A fairly mild current or a small wave is enough to cause problems for a paddler without experience of moving water. Once you understand the behaviour of the water, however, it is possible to cope, and indeed play, with white water rapids that look terrifying to the uninitiated. There is always an element of danger though. A moment's loss of concentration could prove fatal if the proper precautions are not observed.

White water river features demand concentration and proficient paddling skills.

An open-boat canoeist and two kayakers navigate their way around a white water river.

White Water Hydrology

Rapids have a relatively small number of components that always behave in much the same way. Once you can identify and understand these components you are well on the way to being able to master white water paddling.

When you look at a rapid, try not to see it as a whole. The non-paddler looks at white water as one big chaotic mass, when it is in fact made up of separate areas of water that are all fairly constant in their behaviour.

Currents

The water in a river flows predominantly downstream, but there are some parts moving faster than others, and sometimes water even moves upstream. Water in the centre of the river flows quite a bit faster

❱ *A medium-volume and steep white water rapid, Grade (Class) 4.*

Main flow

Micro eddy

Pourover drop

Upstream

Siphon

Stopper or hole

Eddy

Vertical drop

Stopper or hole

Strainer (tree hazard)

Stopper or hole

Eddy

Downstream

Boulder garden

Sloping drop

◔ *Anatomy of a white water river. The current is flowing from right to left. The deepest and strongest part of the downstream flow of water is known as the main flow.*

than water near the banks because of friction with the bank, and because the river is generally deeper in the middle than the shallow margins.

As the river goes around a corner, the fastest part of the current will move towards the outside of the bend. There will still be a zone of slower moving water right next to the outside bank, but it will be narrower, and the slow zone on the inside will be consequently wider.

If the river goes round a very sharp bend, the water cannot flow smoothly around it. This means that the fastest part of the current will collide with the bank on the outside of the bend, and then rebound and continue downstream. Aim to stay in the slower part, which will move in a much more predictable way.

A kayaker reaches over a breaking wave and punches his way through.

Paddling in a large eddy on a pool-drop river. Although the paddler is in relatively calm, or slack, water, it still swirls and moves around him.

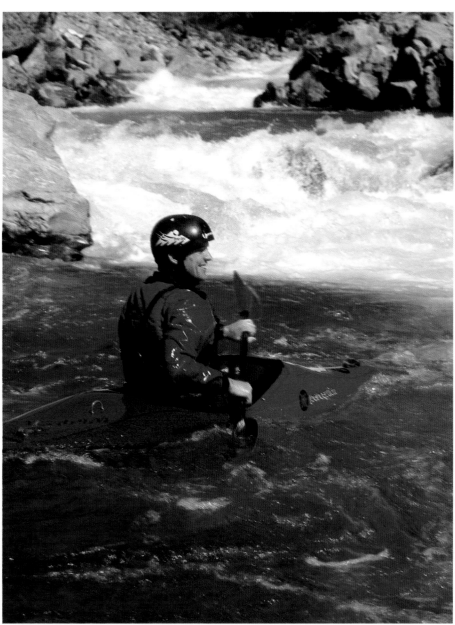

Eddies

If the bank protrudes, a rock breaks the surface, or there is a sharp corner, the water will flow around it and re-circulate upstream to form a sheltered area behind the protrusion or corner. This is called an eddy. It can be flat and calm, or it can rotate strongly, depending on the shape of the feature and the strength of the current. All but the most savagely swirling eddies are good places for kayaks and canoes to rest, regroup, or look for the best route downstream.

Green Water V-shapes

When you look at a rapid you can see that the water flowing between the rocks forms a green water V-shape with its apex pointing downstream. This shows you the path of the deepest and least turbulent current. You can paddle down these Vs, and they are usually the safest route. If this feature is a downstream V, then the V-shaped wakes caused by the rocks are upstream Vs. An upstream V has an obstruction or shallow water at its apex, and should usually be avoided by taking the middle of the downstream V.

The waves that form on either side of the V will meet at the apex and fold over each other to form what is known as a folded or V wave. Since your boat may capsize if you plunge directly into a folded wave, it is sometimes better to leave the V before you hit the apex.

Waves and Hydraulics

If the water flows over a ledge or rock on the bottom of the river, it will cause a disturbance on the surface. What this disturbance looks like to the paddler depends on the shape of the rock, and the depth of water flowing over it.

The more powerful the vertical re-circulation of a water feature, the more it will tend to hold a buoyant object, such as a boat, preventing it from passing through and carrying on downstream. Some people try to differentiate between wave types, but they are all similar phenomena with a profile that varies according to the velocity of the current and the resistance it meets.

When a hydraulic becomes powerful enough to hold a boat, it is often called a stopper or a hole. In extreme cases they can even re-circulate a swimmer. An unbroken wave can also stop a boat if it is big and steep enough, but because it has no component moving upstream, it will never hold a swimmer.

Sometimes the energy of a hydraulic water feature means that instead of one wave, there will be a whole series of them, getting progressively smaller as you go downstream. This is called a wave train, and is usually a bouncy but safe line to take down a rapid. The waves are nearly always pyramidal rather than river wide, and you will get a drier ride by paddling over the corners of waves, so avoiding the deeper middle.

Falls

These are a more dramatic example of the previous phenomena of waves and hydraulics. Where the river drops dramatically, the water will hit the bottom

and rebound upwards. What it does then is dependent on the depth and the steepness of the drop. The more re-circulation and the longer the towback, the more difficult it is for the boater to escape the clutches of the hydraulic.

Back-cut Drops

Certain geological features allow falls to erode in such a way that the water re-circulates behind, as well as downstream of the falls. This forms a double hydraulic from which it may be almost impossible to escape.

Cushions

Where the current rebounds directly off an object in its path, some of the water is forced upwards and some upstream. This forms what is known as a cushion (pillow). Far from being hazardous, these features will usually prevent you from colliding with rocks and walls. However, they can still capsize the unwary, and you should always approach them with caution.

Running a Downstream V

1 When approaching a rapid, look between the rocks and you will see a green water V shape, or "downstream V".

2 A downstream V is where the currents flowing around the rocks converge. This is the least turbulent part of the current.

3 The best route is usually to paddle down the apex of the V, as if it were an arrow pointing out the safest line.

4 There may be extremely turbulent water at the very apex of the V, if it is formed by two waves, as is the case here.

5 Even if the water looks fierce at the apex, this will still be your best route. The water at either side is much worse.

6 This paddler is safely through the V. Downstream Vs rarely point to anything nasty, but be aware that they can.

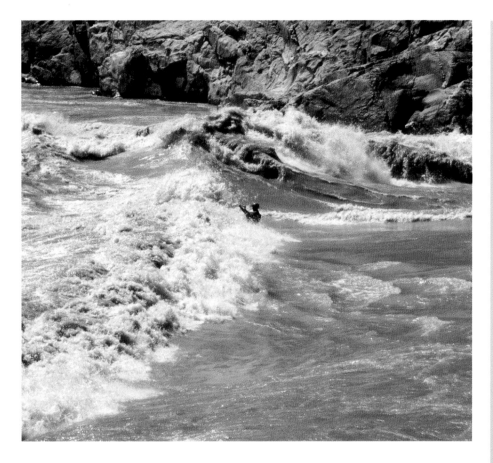

● *On enormous white water the severity of water features is magnified.*

Boils and Seams

Water sometimes wells up from the bottom of the river as it rises to find its way downstream. This forms a feature that would look to a fish's eye like a mushroom, but appears on the surface as an area of elevated, bubbly water that moves outwards from the centre and down at the edges. This is called a boil. Where two or more boils meet, the join, also known as the seam, can be quite accentuated. It can be powerful enough to suck down a swimmer or even an entire boat, but in all but the biggest water this is usually only temporary, and both swimmer and boat will resurface without difficulty after a few seconds.

Whirlpools

The whirlpool is perhaps the most evocative white water feature, but it is also over-rated. It is not nearly as exciting or as dangerous as it seems: only on enormous white water will the whirlpool have the power to do anything more than snatch at the boat, and cause a bit of a wobble, although for paddlers new to white water they are best avoided. Whirlpools occur in areas of adjoining, extremely different phenomena, where there is a high current differential – for instance, along the boundary between an eddy and a strong current. Whirlpools are, unusually, rarely stable features, and they tend to appear at the top of such a boundary and whirl downstream for a few seconds before disappearing altogether.

● *Probably one of the biggest whirlpools ever captured on camera.*

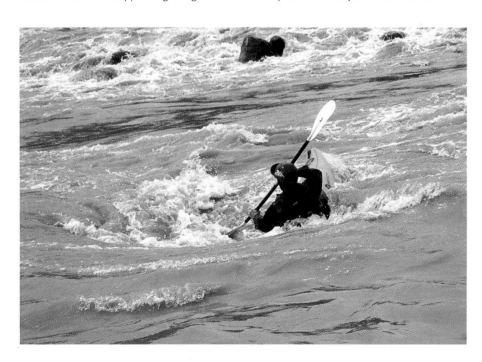

Grading Rivers

It is vitally important that you know how to accurately assess a white water river, and how to fully appreciate someone else's verdict on its safety level. In very extreme cases, it could be the difference between life and death. Always make sure you know your grades.

Grading or classifying white water rivers is essential if you are to assess their severity, and hence their suitability, for your level of paddling. There is a widely accepted international system

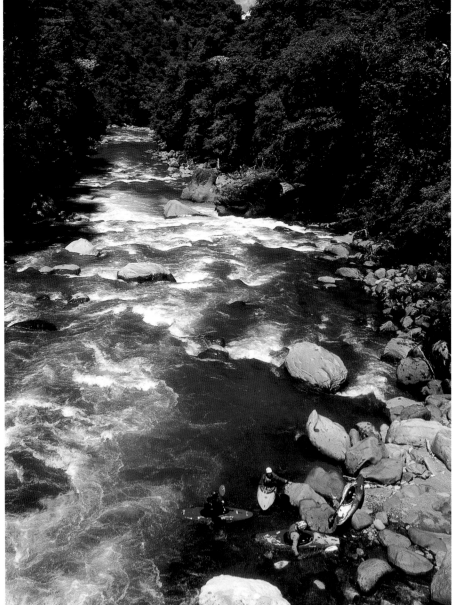

⊙ *A group of paddlers getting out to scout a Grade (Class) 4 rapid on an otherwise Grade 2 or 3 section of river.*

available to all paddlers. However, it is a subjective system that can be open to misinterpretation. As in other areas of paddling, what really counts is your own experience of rivers and your ability to judge a particular river for yourself.

Grades of River

Grade (Class) 1 This is flat water. If the water is moving at all, it has so little energy that the currents can be ignored and they will not affect the boat unduly. Grade 1 rivers are suitable for beginners unless extreme weather has affected the water conditions – for example, if heavy rain has caused flooding.

Grade 2 There may be water currents strong enough to prevent you paddling upstream, or through waves and eddies, but whichever route you take, the rapid will be safe if you have good basic paddling skills.

Grade 3 The waves, currents and eddies will be more pronounced, and there may be obstructions and/or drops that necessitate a particular route down the rapid in order to remain safe and in control of the boat. On Grade 3 water, the safe route should always be obviously visible to the experienced paddler while on his way down the rapid.

Grade 4 There is a safe route down the rapid, but it is not obvious from the boat. The size of the waves and the drops, and the complexity of the rapid, usually dictate that the paddler must first inspect it from the bank in order to plan a safe line and remain in control.

Grade 5 The size and severity of the features, and the complexity of the rapid, has increased to the point where, although there may be a best line through, even that route is not entirely safe, and the paddler can expect to lose control. The rapid is so turbulent and powerful that it is dangerous even for the highly experienced, skilled paddler. Often, swimming in this type of water would result in injury or drowning.

Grade 6 This has always been defined as the upper limit of practicality. There is no safe line to take through the water, and to swim would prove fatal.

⊙ *A big volume Grade 3 rapid such as this calls for experienced handling.*

⊙ *This fairly straightforward rapid is Grade 4 because of the volume and severity of the water.*

Is the System Perfect?

Over time, as boats and skills have constantly improved, many rapids that were once Grade 6 have become widely regarded as a less severe Grade 5; many Grade 4 rapids are now classed as Grade 3, and so on. These revisions make for some confusion in the system.

A number of paddlers have modified the international grading system in an attempt to improve it. Some use a + or – symbol to create more increments, so that 3+ means a difficult Grade 3 river and 5- means a relatively straightforward Grade 5. Some paddlers prefer to add a letter, so that the number indicates the difficulty of paddling the rapid and the letter the level of danger. So 5a would mean "Incredibly hard, but if you swim you will be fine," and 4d would mean "Fairly hard but any kind of mistake would be very dangerous."

None of these alternative, modified systems has gained universal acceptance, however. The original system may have

its problems, but everyone understands it, and it gives a good indication of what you can expect to find. The most important point is that you are able to look at a rapid and accurately assess it, knowing the likely consequences of tackling it given your paddling ability and that of the rest of your group.

Tackling White Water

Before you attempt to tackle white water, you must understand the river grading system. If you are new to paddling rapids, do not attempt anything over Grade 2, particularly until you have learnt to roll. As you gain confidence, you can build up to more difficult rapids, but it should be a progressive development. You will also need all the strokes that will be outlined in this section. Being able to roll well is important as you are likely to capsize, but you are unlikely to roll successfully every time (initially, at least), so be prepared for a swim. Above all, be confident: an anxious boater is never a good boater. Facing and overcoming challenges is part of any adventure sport, but you should not attempt anything if you are not comfortable with the possible outcome.

⊙ *This massive waterfall is ungradeable because of its power. To run it would probably result in death: the paddler's skill and route would make no difference.*

WHITE WATER EQUIPMENT

The minimum equipment you need for tackling white water will include a boat, paddle, spraydeck (spray skirt), if paddling in a kayak, flotation device and helmet. You should also have a throw-line, and a knife that can be used to cut the throw-line in an emergency. Many people paddle with only the minimum amount of equipment, and find their paddling all the more enjoyable for not being weighed down with extraneous items, some of which they are unlikely to ever need.

On the other hand, there are many other pieces of equipment that can be useful, important or even essential, depending on the conditions you are likely to encounter on the water. In the following chapter, we outline the types of equipment that are commonly used by white water paddlers today, and discuss when they are required and why. Deciding how much equipment you need is a personal choice, and it should always be based on your own needs and experiences.

A well-equipped paddler in a modern white water kayak.

Airbags lashed in place on a modern white water open canoe.

Kayaks for White Water

A kayak for white water paddling will usually be made of plastic, unless it is designed for a specialist discipline such as slalom, white water racing, or squirt boating. It should have enough buoyancy to float well even when completely full of water. If there is any significant risk that, when full of water, you might end up swimming out of your boat (and there is a risk unless you are highly skilled), you should also fit airbags inside the boat to minimize the amount of water that can enter. Airbags are inflatable PVC bags designed to keep water out of the boat in the event of swamping.

Choosing a Kayak

Most people are now introduced to white water in a boat that is about 2.5m (8½ft) long, and fairly flat-bottomed. Many older books and some instructors still regard boats that are 4m (13ft) long and round-hulled as more suitable, but beginners and experienced paddlers alike will benefit from the responsiveness of a short boat. Also, the more volume the boat has, the better it will respond in white water, but it should not be so huge that the paddler can not properly reach the water when seated.

The boat must have strong footrests with some shock absorption system, and a back strap to support the back and maintain a spinal "S". The boat should also be equipped with end grabs strong enough to take a 1,000kg (2,200lb) load,

◔ *A heavy-duty, reinforced white water paddle with a symmetrical blade. This is a good, affordable solution as a first white water paddle.*

and should be padded inside as much as is necessary to fit the paddler exactly. A boat that does not fit you is no fun at all.

Kayak Paddles

White water paddles are shorter than flat water paddles – a typical length is 1.9–1.98m (6ft 2in–6ft 7in). Many older books recommend longer paddles, and in 1975, white water kayakers were using paddles 2.1–2.2m (6ft 10in–7ft 2in) long, but they were also using 4m (13ft) kayaks. Things have changed since then. In today's short

◔ *A lightweight carbon fibre white water paddle with an asymmetrical blade. Lighter and stronger, this is the choice of the white water expert.*

boats, shorter paddles mean faster paddle strokes and therefore more responsive paddling.

The paddle must be strong enough to survive being smashed against rocks, and it should be stiff enough to provide good feedback from the water. Good models can be expensive, but their superior performance and durability justify the cost.

◔ *This boat has been fitted with thigh grips, a back strap and foam padding to ensure the paddler fits snugly and cannot move inside the boat.*

◔ *A modern white water kayak suitable for beginners. However, an expert could tackle all but the most extreme white water in this boat with further outfitting.*

❷ The Perception Dancer, an early modern white water kayak, first built in 1979. At 3.7m (12ft) in length, this boat changed the widely held belief that kayaks needed to be 4m (13ft) long. In fact, 4m (13ft) was originally a slalom kayak dimension designed to limit performance, not to enhance it.

❷ This 3m (10ft) Pyranha kayak is short enough to be versatile but long enough for touring. Hence, it represents the modern general-purpose kayak, suitable for white water if correctly equipped.

❷ This all-round white water kayak is only 2.3m (7½ft) in length, and has a flat-bottomed, planing hull design. It could be used for paddling rapids or for freestyle or play paddling, and is outfitted to a high standard. An expert might use this craft on extreme white water but, ultimately, its low volume and pointed ends make it less safe on steep rivers.

❷ At 2.4m (8ft) long and with high-volume, rounded ends, this kayak is designed for extreme white water. The ends are unlikely to submerge easily and will resist entrapment. The boat will perform better when laden with equipment, and the narrow hull will soften the impact of waterfalls.

❷ This inflatable kayak may look less functional, but it is suited to running hard rapids. With the aid of thigh straps you can lock yourself in, just as you can in a more rigid boat.

Canoes for White Water

Canoes for white water paddling have more variations in design than kayaks. Open boats can be made from fibreglass, but are more usually polyethylene plastic or a sandwich of plastics with a core. The latter can give incredible durability with excellent stiffness and low weight.

On an easy stretch of white water, open canoeists might risk paddling without any special equipment, ensuring only that the boat has enough buoyancy to float when it is full of water. More often, though, every bit of the boat not occupied by the crew will be filled with airbags or rigid buoyancy barrels (very good for storing additional gear), which are lashed in place with cords or webbing. The conventional canoe seat or thwart can be replaced by a foam saddle, which might even have thigh straps to hold you in place. This enables the open canoe to be rolled like a decked boat should it capsize.

◔ *An open boat canoe is packed with air bags, which will keep it afloat when swamped with water.*

◔ *A white water canoe paddle, made from Carbon-Kevlar™ and fibreglass.*

◔ *A white water freestyle canoe. This boat is designed for play paddling, but could be used as well for running rapids.*

◔ *A typical white water canoe is characterized by its short length, rounded ends and continuous rocker.*

On white water, every bit of space in the boat is filled with airbags, which are lashed in place with cord.

All white water canoes feature saddle seats, as well as footrests behind the seat for use when kneeling.

Open boaters often carry throw-lines attached to the ends of the boat. In the event of a swim, which is very likely because open canoes are quite hard to roll, the paddler can swim to the bank holding the end of the line, and then brace himself until the boat swings into the bank. This can be better than trying to swim with such a large boat in the rapid.

Open or Decked?

The first decision is whether to choose a decked or open canoe. The decked canoe is basically a kayak with a seat, footrest, and its back rest replaced by a saddle and straps. There are very few purpose-built decked canoes today, except for hand-built composite slalom boats. Most recreational and freestyle white water paddlers use a kayak shell which they transform into a canoe.

Often the body position in a decked canoe is further forward than it would be in the equivalent kayak, because the paddler's legs are in a kneeling position and not in front of him. This can mean that the canoeist needs a special spraydeck (spray skirt) made with the body tube further forward. Always check that the hole for your waist is in the right place for the seat in your boat!

Canoe Paddles

Just like kayak paddles, canoe paddles for white water need to be strong, light, and stiff enough to provide good

feedback. A little flexibility is important because it allows the paddle to absorb shocks and prevent muscle strain; too much flexibility, on the other hand, will be counter-productive to your efforts.

Nowadays most canoe paddles are made from composite materials such as fibreglass, carbon or Kevlar™. There are traditionalists who prefer the warmth and feedback that comes from a wooden paddle, but wooden paddles are very high maintenance in a white water

environment. The cheapest paddles have ABS plastic blades on a metal tubular shaft. These will certainly do the job for a quarter of the price of some models, and would be suitable for beginners who may not progress far with white water. However, they don't deliver much power or feedback from the water. They can also snap easily, especially in cold conditions.

A tandem open canoe breaking into the current on a white water river.

Accessories and Clothing for White Water

On white water you need heavy duty gear to keep you dry in turbulent water, and to protect you from injury and drowning.

Spraydecks

Spraydecks (spray skirts) for kayaks and decked canoes are absolutely essential in rough water. Spraydecks are invariably made from neoprene, the same material that is used for wetsuits. Fabric spraydecks used for flat water are splash-proof rather than waterproof, and will not be adequate for white water.

A good neoprene spraydeck will keep out every drop of water, and will not come off the cockpit rim unless you pull hard on the release strap, which is usually located at the front. Some basic spraydecks are available for the less confident paddler, which will come free if you kick and twist them, but that means they will probably come off in a roll or heavy waves. To see how secure the spraydeck is, put it on your empty boat, then put your hand in through the tube and under the deck, and lift up the boat by the spraydeck. If it stays on, it can be used on serious white water.

Whichever spraydeck you get, make sure that you can release it easily using the strap provided: practise doing this on white water as well as flat. When putting the spraydeck on, always check that the release strap is not trapped inside.

Flotation

Make sure that the flotation you use is intended for white water. For severe white water, some paddlers use special aids with a quick-release chest belt in case they need to be rescued. However, you should only get one of these if you know how to use one. Otherwise it is more likely to endanger than save you.

White water flotation aids can be minimal and slimline, as favoured by freestyle and play paddlers, or bulky and more buoyant, for tackling extreme rapids. The choice is determined by the likelihood of being capsized. The freestyle aids will allow more freedom, and you will be able to paddle better, but they might not afford you enough support if you are swimming in heavily aerated water.

◉ *This reinforced white water buoyancy aid (personal flotation device) is fitted with a chest belt for use in a rescue situation. The belt should only be used by paddlers who have been trained in white water rescue.*

◉ *A white water play paddler equipped for summer: note the short-sleeved shell and wetsuit shorts. The flotation device, helmet and high-performance spraydeck (skirt) should be worn in all weathers.*

◉ *A reinforced white water spraydeck made from neoprene, the minimum quality material for white water paddling. The tight-fitting body tube is pulled right up to prevent water getting into the boat.*

◉ *A white water river running outfit. With the harness flotation aid, wetsuit trousers and a long-sleeved drytop, this paddler is equipped for extreme white water in any weather.*

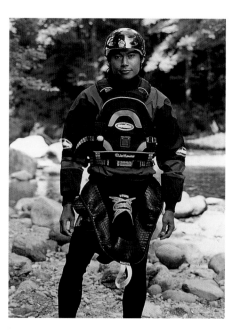

Helmet

All white water paddlers are advised to wear helmets because of the high risk of finding yourself in the water, and knocking your boat or yourself against rocks. Choose a good-quality model that will protect your temples and forehead. Make sure the helmet fits well and will not come off, fall over your eyes, or expose the base of your skull to an impact. Remember, too, that the bigger the helmet, the more it can wrench your head around when you are upside down.

There used to be a fashion for having drainage holes in a helmet to let out any water that gets in during a capsize or roll.

⬇ *Some people use all-in-one drysuits for cold weather paddling, but the zipper can be an encumbrance and the suit lacks many of the features of the drytop.*

Many books still in circulation recommend that you only use a helmet with drainage holes. However, modern helmets are now padded with closed-cell foam. This stops the water getting in, and it means there is less chance of anything (such as an overhanging tree branch) poking through one of the holes. Foam-lined helmets are also warmer.

Clothing

In hot weather, the main purpose of clothing on the upper body is to keep water from entering the spraydeck tube, and protect you from the sun. In colder climes or on cold water, you may need several layers of clothing to keep warm.

Most boaters today use a specially designed paddling jacket, called a cagoule or cag. For warmer weather, there is a short-sleeve version. Cags usually have a seal at the neck and wrists to keep out water, the ultimate being an efficient latex dry seal. Good cags have a double waist system that sandwiches your spraydeck. They are made from a breathable, waterproof fabric, which will cut down on perspiration.

How much insulation you wear under your paddling jacket is up to you, but you will not need much. White water boating is extremely vigorous, and if you wear a thick fleece you will overheat in no time. One or two light to midweight layers should suffice, even in cold weather.

Wetsuits

Beginners to white water often wear wetsuits to keep them warm and protect them from knocks. A popular wetsuit is the long-john design, which allows the upper body freedom of movement. More confident paddlers may find this wetsuit too restricting, preferring wetsuit shorts, wetsuit trousers, or thermal leggings with dry or semi-dry over-trousers, according to the weather and water conditions.

Footwear

Your choice of footwear for white water paddling needs to have a good sole for scrambling about on wet, slippery rocks. Some paddlers choose wetsuit boots, some prefer special watersports shoes, and others wear technical sandals, with or without wetsuit socks. Be aware that anything that is not strapped firmly to your feet is likely to get sucked off during a white water swim.

FREESTYLE

Some freestyle boats are so slimline that you cannot get in wearing bulky footwear. Yet these boats are paddled on white water, so what do freestylers wear on their feet? The point here is that you would only be paddling the more vulnerable freestyle boat in the first place if you were an experienced paddler and within your personal limits. Freestyle boaters usually wear either wetsuit socks or go barefoot, with a pair of sandals or shoes tied in the back of the boat for when they are back on shore.

Safety and Rescue Equipment

There are a number of pieces of rescue equipment that are specially designed for white water use, and all kayakers who intend to paddle rapids should have a basic understanding of their use. There are four essential pieces of equipment that you require.

Throw-line

A throw-line is an invaluable piece of white water equipment. Practise with it until you are confident you could use it in an emergency: the throw-line is next to useless unless it is deployed correctly.

A throw-line is a rescue rope. It consists of a length of rope that will float tied to a bag. The bag will often have some foam buoyancy to keep it afloat as well.

In order to rescue someone who is swimming after a capsize, take your throw-line, open the bag and grasp the loose end of the rope, and throw the bag to the victim. Modern throw-lines are superbly designed so that they fly a

⊙ *A throw-line is attached to a rescue belt flotation aid using a karabiner.*

⊙ *The throw-line is an essential piece of rescue equipment.*

long way with the rope running out smoothly behind. Aim to land the bag beyond the swimmer, so that the rope falls across him, and he can grab it and be pulled to safety.

In theory, this would appear simple, but it can be a tricky procedure when the water is moving fast, particularly if the victim panics. This is why it is imperative that all paddlers practise being both victim and rescuer, and are able to throw and catch the line. Always read the instructions that come with the throw-line.

Flotation

A buoyancy aid (personal flotation device) used for flat water is not appropriate for white water. White water models are sometimes fitted with a rescue belt, which can be an advantage to the trained user in extremely severe rescue situations.

The purpose of the quick-release rescue belt is to allow for a line to be attached to the back of the buoyancy aid, so that the wearer can attempt a rescue with someone holding the other end of the rope. Because the rescuer might also get into difficulties, it is essential that he can release himself using the quick-release buckle fitted to the front of the belt.

The line is attached to the back of the rescue belt. This is so that the wearer would remain the right way up, and able to breathe, if held in a fast-flowing current at the end of a line. Bear in mind that not all white water flotation aids are well designed. Take care when faced with a selection of models: choose one that you know works well for rescues.

Another common problem is that white water flotation aids often rely on the rescue belt to give them a good fit. Before you buy, make sure the aid fits well when the chest belt is unfastened. Otherwise, you may find yourself swimming in an ill-fitting buoyancy aid, just when you need it most.

Slings, Karabiners and Pulleys

A sling can be used as a towing aid and for securing boats. Made from reinforced nylon webbing,

⊙ *Karabiners: the chunky screw-gate (here, the pink ones) and the quicker but less secure snap-gate (the blue).*

⊙ *Climbing slings are very useful for towing and securing boats and paddles.*

❶ *(Below) A pruning saw is a fantastic tool on the river. This cheap garden tool will cut through quite large branches and strong plastic with equal ease. Be careful to get one that can be locked closed, as the blade is a really nasty piece of work.*

❶ *A typical folding river knife. This one has a serrated part to the blade for hacking at difficult jobs, such as tree branches.*

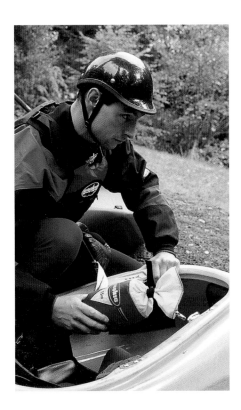

slings are extremely strong but occupy very little space in the boat. If you also have a karabiner – a lightweight alloy coupling link – it will make the sling easier to deploy for securing and towing boats. Karabiners can have a screw-gate or a snap-gate fastening, and you should try to include one of each. Some karabiners are big enough to close around a paddle shaft: these are the most useful because you can use them to secure or tow paddles.

If you have a sling and a couple of karabiners you can use them together to make a pulley for your throw-line rope. In some situations, such as when a boat has become lodged between rocks after a capsize, a pulley system, operated from the river bank, will be your best chance of recovering the boat. Special pulleys for white water rescue are available, and they are more effective, but your boating will be turning into quite an operation if you get to this stage. For advice on how to work a pulley system, see *White Water Safety and Rescue.*

Knives and Saws

Whenever you take a rope with you as part of your safety and rescue equipment, you should also take a knife to cut it with. Small folding knives are the best because they are extremely sharp, but are still small enough to be carried in the pocket of most buoyancy aids. Some white water paddlers carry fixed-blade diving knives, but these can easily cause accidental injuries, and because they are much heavier they will quickly sink if you drop them in the water.

An ordinary garden pruning saw does not weigh too much, and is invaluable for cutting away branches of trees, which are the white water paddler's worst nightmare. They can also be used in more extreme cases – for example, to free a boater who has become trapped by a fallen tree branch.

❶ *(Top) The throw-line can be stowed inside the kayak or decked canoe.*

❶ *On an open canoe, the throw-line can be attached to the ends.*

Using a Throw-line

1 Get to the shore and out of your boat. Standing on the river bank, undo the bag of your throw-line and pull out about 2m (6½ft) of rope.

2 Identify where the swimmer is and throw the bag (NOT the rope) to them. Aim for somewhere behind them, so that the rope falls over their head.

3 Bring the rope from the swimmer, around the back of you and over your shoulder. Lean back and take the strain as the swimmer swings into the bank.

WHITE WATER SKILLS

This chapter provides a guide to the fundamental skills required to paddle through rapids. There are a few basic tips that can make a big difference to how well you cope with the transition from flat water to rapids. Having read the section on white water hydrology, you will understand that many forces are acting on the boat. Anticipation is the key to remaining in control. If you react to the water, your actions will always be too late. You must lean, edge and use the paddle, anticipating what the water will do. This comes only with experience.

Where you look is where you go. If you want your boat to change direction, rotate your body and look at your new goal to make it easier to turn the boat. The exception to this is rolling, when the body will follow the boat out of the water.

To be successful you also need to be aggressive. White water does not reward defensive behaviour. If you shy away from a wave or a rock, it will tip you in. Turn your shoulder and lean aggressively towards it, and you will survive the problem.

Finally, do not start doing something if you have not got a fixed goal. If you leave the safety of an eddy, you should know where the next safe place is, and be confident that you can get there. If you head down river without a plan, you are likely to run into trouble.

◀ A group of experienced paddlers enjoying big and bouncy white water rapids.

▼ Novice kayakers learning their first white water skills under expert supervision.

Planning your White Water Trip

Before you paddle on white water it is extremely important to know and understand what you are getting into. You can at best have a bad day, and at worst come to some serious harm if you misinterpret its nature and severity.

In the enthusiastic rush to get on the water, it is very tempting to overlook certain basic safety requirements. These include making sure everyone in the group knows the plan for the trip, who is carrying what in terms of safety and rescue equipment, provisions and maps, and where the dry clothes are at the end of the journey.

Pre-trip Preparation

Everyone going out on the water should understand the basic principles of white water hydrology and the international grading system. Someone in the paddling group (preferably everyone, but this is not always possible) must be experienced enough to be able to judge the grade of water, and whether it is suitable for everyone in the party. Finally, if parts of the river are too difficult for people in the group, will they be able to stop, get out and walk around the section?

◐ Preparing for a trip on white water. Lay out the equipment on the ground, and check off everything you will need.

Everyone should also know how long the trip is going to last, so that they can bring appropriate amounts of food, drink and equipment. It might be a quick 20-minute blast down an exciting section of river, or a trip lasting a few days with camping on the river bank. The type of provisions and extra clothing needed will also depend on the weather, so listen to a reliable daily weather report for the area before you set out.

Shuttles

A white water trip is usually a one way journey because the water flows too fast for there to be any possibility of paddling back to the starting point. Your group may be fortunate enough to be delivered to the put-in and collected from the take-out (also known as the egress), but more usually the group will have to give some thought to the procedure known as the "shuttle". Here is how it works.

The group convenes at the put-in to unload their boats and the equipment they will need on the river. All the dry clothes and anything that will not be required until the end of the trip, including towels and hot drinks, is loaded into one or more vehicles, which are driven to the get-out point. The drivers of these vehicles now need to get back to the put-in, so one extra vehicle will have to

◐ Before you get afloat, make sure everyone knows the plan for the trip.

accompany them and bring everyone back, unless you are lucky enough to have the help of a non-paddling driver, known to boaters as a "shuttle-bunny".

It may be practical to walk back to the put-in, which means that no vehicles are left at the top of the river and you won't need to return there afterwards. Otherwise, when the trip is over, someone will have to take the shuttle driver back to his car. Remember, all the dry clothes should remain at the get-out point until everyone has finished the trip.

If you don't have a shuttle-bunny at the get-out, it is essential that the paddlers carry with them the keys for all cars left there. It is all too common to leave the keys in the car left at the put-in, and then have to go on a long and arduous mission to recover them at the end. This can be extremely unpopular with a group of cold and tired paddlers whose warm clothes are safely locked away!

Safety Measures

Make sure that everyone knows the plan, and who is responsible for what during the trip. In a group of experienced paddlers who know each other well, there will not be any formalities because everyone knows what to do, but in a mixed-abilities group, it is important to have a preliminary talk before you set out.

An experienced group member must run through the procedure for the trip, emphasizing where you will re-group, who will go first and last, and who has the essential safety equipment. Typically the strongest and/or most experienced paddlers will go first and last, taking the basic items of rescue equipment. At least three members of the party (if not everyone) should carry throw-lines.

Finally, the entire group should warm-up and stretch at the same time. This means that everyone is ready together and you won't have some getting cold and stiff while others are still getting ready.

Communication

Hand signals can be used between paddlers for communication. This should not be attempted while paddling, but it is useful if paddlers have stopped in separate eddies because the noise of the river can preclude verbal communication. Some books describe a "correct" signalling procedure, but different groups use different signals. Discuss the signals the group will use during the pre-trip talk.

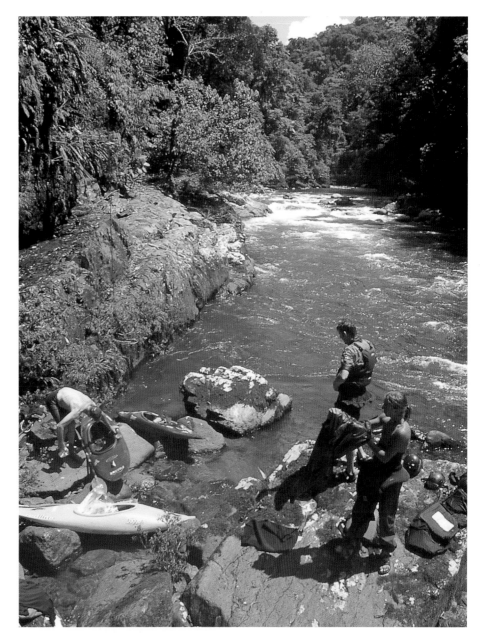

❱ *A group of paddlers get out of the water for a meeting in a remote gorge.*

❰ *These paddlers are discussing the plan for the next section of their trip.*

Launching into White Water

There are several options when it comes to launching a boat, including techniques for entering the water from banks 10m (33ft) high. Build up your launching skills gradually. If you attempt an ambitious technique you are not ready for, you are likely to get hurt.

Getting into the water can be trickier than you might think. Unless there is an area of slow-moving flat water at the put-in, it will be impossible to get into the boat by the usual means. Kayak paddlers will find it difficult to put on their neoprene spraydecks (spray skirts) while afloat, and it will be difficult for anyone to get settled in the boat and not get swept away while trying to arrange their equipment. One of several techniques will be required.

Launching in an Eddy

If there is a convenient eddy at the put-in, it may be possible to put your boat in the water, get in, and put on spraydecks before pushing off. However, even the gentlest eddies are not usually stationary, and the water will be trying to carry you upstream and feed you into the current before you are ready. You will therefore need someone to hold your boat while you get in and put on your deck, making sure that your paddle does not float away.

❯ *Seal launching a kayak off a low river bank on to flat water.*

❮ *Getting into a white water open canoe on a section of slack water.*

Seal Launching

Because getting into the boat in an eddy is sometimes impossible, and since most paddlers prefer to be independent, it is normally better to get into the boat and get everything in place on dry land, and then launch yourself into the water. This technique is called a seal launch. No-one seems to know whether this refers to the way a seal slides into the sea from a rock, or the fact that the paddler is sealed in the boat as it is launched.

How you launch is determined by the bank, the depth of the water, and the nature of the river downstream. If there is a gently shelving slope into the water, you can get in the boat at the water's edge and push yourself into the water. If the water is moving fast, it may be better to launch backwards because the current will spin the boat around, pointing it upstream as you go in. This is a better orientation for getting away from the bank.

If there is a vertical drop from the bank to the water that is not too big, it is often better to shuffle to the edge sideways, and then lean out until you can bump the boat off the ledge with your hips, landing flat in the water. It takes practice to do this without falling in, so try it in deep, safe water at first. It is not comfortable or safe to use this method from a height of more than 1m (3½ft), unless the water is extremely aerated.

◔ *A canoe can be seal launched off a bank as easily as a kayak.*

◔ *Launching sideways off a low wall. This is a better solution if the water is too shallow for a vertical dive.*

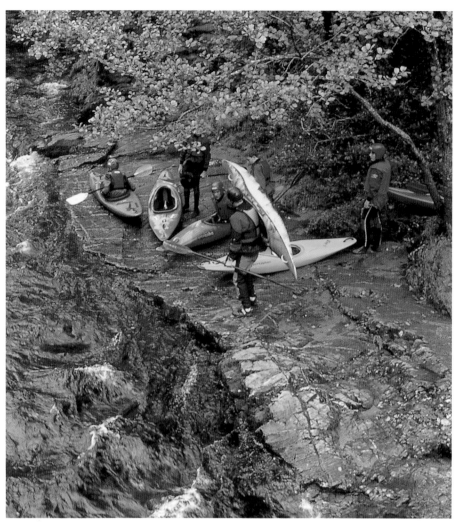

◔ *Making an enormous vertical seal launch. This kind of thing should only ever be attempted out of necessity.*

If the drop from the river bank is larger than 1m (3½ft) or not quite vertical you will have to launch forwards. This may involve free-falling, bow first, into the water, so you will need to make sure that the water is deep enough. Stick your paddle into the water to measure the depth: if it is less than 1m (3½ft) deep you risk injury from hitting the bottom. Push yourself to the edge using the paddle on one side and your free hand on the other, then launch yourself off the bank with a shove, bringing the other hand on to the paddle as you fall.

The push off is important because if you topple slowly you will over-rotate, and might land on your head. Sit fairly upright, and do not hold the paddle in front of your face in case it hits you in the nose. People have been known to seal launch safely from heights of up to 18m (60ft) this way, but try it initially from no more than 3m (10ft) because it can be difficult to maintain the correct posture while performing the manoeuvre.

◔ *Getting a group into their boats on a rock ledge. When they are all ready to go, they will slide off into the rapid.*

If you have to launch from a great height but the water is not deep enough for a vertical entry, you still have a few options. You can either shove off hard from the bank, or get someone to give you a push, so that you enter the water at a shallower angle; this can be tricky. Or you can drop into the water sideways and land flat, provided you feel that your fitness or the aeration of the water means that you can exceed the 1m (3½ft) rule without injuring yourself; this is more risky. Or you can drop in sideways, letting the boat land on its side if you have the skill to do this. If you attempt this, do not land with a lot of force on your paddle blade. Even if the paddle does not touch the bottom you can hurt your shoulder, and you might break the paddle. It is better to capsize than to find yourself stranded or injured.

Breaking Out Techniques

The break out is a manoeuvre that allows you to move the boat out of the current and into an eddy whenever you want to take a break from the fast-moving water.

The eddy will be divided from the main flow of the river by an eddy-line. This is a distinct line or interface between the water moving downstream and the water in the eddy, which is stationary or is moving more slowly upstream.

As the boat crosses the eddy-line the current will try to spin the boat around and tip it over. In order to counter this it is important to lean the boat upstream, i.e. into the turn, as it crosses the line.

It is usually advisable to paddle into the eddy while pointing downstream, and allow the current to spin the boat to face upriver. This makes it easy to enter the top of the eddy, a relatively safe and predictable place, and to leave it again to proceed downstream. However, it is

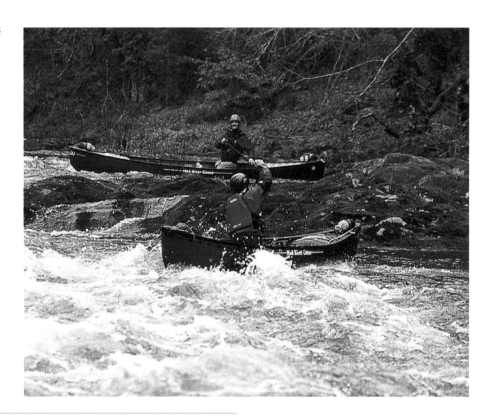

Breaking Out using a Bow Rudder

1 Aim to get the bow into the top of the eddy at an angle of 45°.

2 Plant the bow rudder firmly in the eddy and lean the boat upstream.

3 Hang on the bow rudder until the boat is completely in the eddy.

4 Turn the rudder into a power stroke to pull you back up the eddy, if required.

🔵 *Two canoeists negotiate their way down the river from one eddy to another.*

possible to paddle into the eddy across the current, or even while pointing upstream if necessary. The crucial point is to maintain that upstream lean once in the eddy.

It is best to approach the eddy at some speed, and to perform a powerful sweep stroke on the downstream side as you cross the eddy-line to ensure that you cross it properly and do not hang about at the interface, which can be a difficult place even for experts. As the boat turns into the eddy and you apply or increase your lean, you should support yourself with a low brace for stability, and to ensure that the boat carries on turning the right way. You should finish up well inside the eddy-line, facing upstream, and with the bow of the boat close to the top of the eddy.

With a good technique it is possible to enter the eddy without doing any strokes at all, just relying on the edges and carving performance of the boat to give you the necessary drive and turning force.

Exactly what type of stroke you use to break out is up to you. You should be

Breaking Out using a Low Brace

1 Aim the bow into the top of the eddy at 45°, and low brace on the upstream side.

2 As the boat begins to turn, lean on the low brace fairly hard.

comfortable with all the strokes by the time you venture out on to white water for the first time, so with any luck it will come naturally. Remember, though, that it is the difference in current as you cross the eddy-line that turns the boat and not your stroke.

The advantage of a low brace as you cross the eddy-line is that it will provide the greatest support. It is also an easy stroke to apply in what is (to the novice) an uncertain situation; as a result it is quite common to see paddlers new to white water using the low brace.

The advantage of using a bow rudder stroke is that it can be feathered to apply only as much braking force as required (which means it need not slow the boat), yet it still provides support to the confident paddler, and can feather into a forward stroke to take you deeper into the eddy as you come to a halt. The bow rudder would be the stroke of choice for experienced paddlers when breaking in or out of a current on white water.

To break out with no paddle strokes is good practice and helps you to feel the effect the water has on the hull, uncluttered as you are with feedback from the paddle. When you are entirely confident at moving around on a rapid, breaking with no brace can be used as a training exercise to maintain your concentration and control.

Breaking Out with No Brace

1 Attack the eddy at 45°, as when using a low brace.

2 Lean upstream a little before you start to turn the boat.

GO WITH THE FLOW

A white water river is primarily made up of water currents and eddies. It is up to the paddler to use these forces to manoeuvre and stop the boat. Entering currents, stopping the boat in case of a problem, to take a rest or to look at something interesting, and navigating your way across a river are vital skills that you need to learn to stay in control of your boat, and to enjoy your time on white water.

3 Hold the lean and keep believing it is going to work!

4 Finish facing upstream, and don't level the boat until you have stopped turning.

Breaking In Techniques

The technique for entering the river current from an eddy and proceeding downstream is known as breaking in. It is precisely the opposite of beaking out.

Paddle into the current while pointing slightly upstream, and with enough speed to ensure that you make it completely into the flow. As with breaking out, use a powerful forward sweep on the upstream side to drive the bow into the current and initiate the turn. Then use a low brace or similarly supportive turning stroke on the downstream side to complete the turn. Clearly, the forces here are acting the other way, so the current will be trying to tip you upstream. You must lean quite decisively downstream, again into the turn, supporting yourself with your turning stroke, until you are well into the current.

If there are waves in the main flow, you will do better to enter the current in a trough rather than on the peak of a wave.

As with the breaking out technique, there are a number of ways that you can achieve your goal of crossing the eddy-line into the current. The safest and most reliable way at first, when you are first learning to break in, is to use a low brace. Start off by paddling up the eddy fast enough to allow you to make it across the eddy-line: you need to do your low brace as, or slightly before, the boat

crosses the line and starts to turn. If you are paddling too slowly, you will spin around to face the downstream right on the eddy-line, and you will probably fall into the water. However, it is incorrect to paddle across the eddy-line and then turn. This feels all wrong, and it doesn't put you in a good position in the rapid either.

⬤ *The important thing about breaking in is to make it into the flow, where you can establish a safe line downstream.*

More experienced paddlers tend to do exactly the same thing but using a bow rudder stroke in place of the low brace. This has the advantage that if you are not going quite fast enough, or if you

Breaking In using a Low Brace

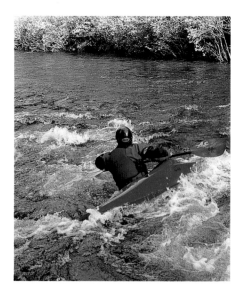

1 Paddle up to the top of the eddy-line. Make your last stroke on the current side.

2 Your next stroke will be a sweep to drive you into the flow and start the turn.

3 Place the low brace on the downstream side for support as you make the turn.

turn too much, your paddle blade is ready for a forward stroke, sweep stroke or support stroke, responding to what the current is doing and making sure you complete the turn while making it into the flow of the current. The only difference is that you should reach forwards to place the bow rudder in the current because this stroke will not always slice cleanly

across the eddy-line without snagging in the water or tipping you right in.

Experienced paddlers may break into the current without using a turning/bracing stroke. This is rather like the technique for breaking out with no brace, which is not a stroke but an exercise. In the case of breaking in, the paddler would appear to paddle across the

🔼 *Breaking in below a small drop and immediately lining up for the next one.*

eddy-line, which is bad technique. A paddler with excellent balance and control may be able to cross the eddy-line and turn, while appearing to paddle forwards, but do not attempt this until you have the skill and experience to do it well.

Break in using a Bow Rudder

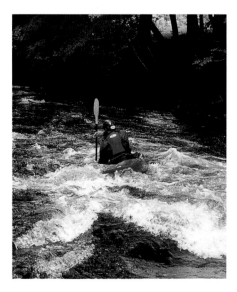

1 Paddle out of the top of the eddy at 45°, lifting the upstream edge of the boat.

2 Make a bow rudder on the downstream side and lean on the stroke.

3 Hold the stroke until you are pointing downstream, then start paddling again.

Ferry Glide

Sometimes you will want to paddle across the current without turning downstream, often from an eddy to a point on the other side. This is known as a ferry glide, named after the ferry boats that used to cross rivers attached to a fixed wire. This does not involve a wire, but you have to paddle fast enough to stop being swept away. The skill of maintaining the correct angle is just the same as the ferryman's.

Ferry gliding is a very useful skill for crossing fast rivers, and for moving into a better position in the current. It can also be done in reverse, so that you move across the current while still facing downstream as you look for the best line down a rapid.

You need to keep the boat pointing upstream. The faster the current and the more its speed varies across the flow, the more directly upstream you will need to aim. Rather than keeping it on track by using forward sweeps on the downstream side to stop the boat from spinning around, you should lift your upstream edge. Use your knee rather than leaning your body downstream, and keep paddling hard enough so that you move across the current without being carried downstream. If you are entering an eddy on the other side, you will need to release your edge and lean slightly upstream as you cross the eddy-line.

If you find that the boat tries to turn downstream, you were not pointing upstream enough. Forward sweep the bow aggressively back into line to recover. However, anticipation is always better than reaction. It tends to go wrong only because you didn't set the correct angle of attack. Getting the angle exactly right only comes with experience. Initially, the rule of thumb is to set off pointing as directly upstream as you can while still allowing you to get across the eddy-line.

Reverse Ferry Glide

The ferry glide can also be done in reverse, so that you move across the current while still facing downstream, as you look for the best line down a rapid. The reverse ferry glide is an essential skill in white water paddling because many rivers have sections that can only be paddled in reverse. Unlike many reverse skills, it is actually easier in many ways to keep the boat tracking across the current than it would be when ferry gliding forwards, although all paddlers have less boat control when paddling backwards.

Ferry Glide Technique

1 As you leave the eddy, point as far upstream as you can while still making it across the eddy-line.

2 Lift the upstream – eddy side – edge of the boat as you cross the eddy-line into the main current.

3 Keep paddling, adjusting your angle across the current as needed.

4 As you reach the other side of the eddy, change edges as you cross the eddy-line by lifting the downstream edge.

5 Enter the other eddy in the same way as you would if you were breaking out.

6 You can now continue to paddle your way up the eddy.

S-cross

If the current is too fast to ferry glide, and the eddy-line is too difficult to negotiate, or the target eddy is a little downstream from your starting point, you can try a modified ferry glide called a cross. This involves letting the boat turn enough so that you ensure a fast transit across the current, at the expense of being carried downstream a short distance. In extreme cases this becomes an S-cross; the boat is allowed to break in until it is travelling directly across the current, then you immediately change to a break out to enter the target eddy, making an S shape across the river.

The S-cross as a set piece is used more for practice than anything else. However, learning to S-cross accurately from one eddy to another on a rapid will give you a lot of confidence in your ability to navigate white water, and will help you combine your repertoire of different skills and manoeuvres into a seamless flow. You will find this technique extremely useful when eddy-hopping your way down an unknown rapid, when you want to get from one safe eddy to another without having to think too hard about how to go about it.

If you attack the eddy-lines at speed, the boat can be made to plane and jet across narrow currents very quickly indeed. It will need practice and excellent reflexes to change edges at just the right time. If you cross a wider current like this, the boat will quickly stop planing and you will be in a conventional ferry glide. If this is not what you want, make sure you attack wider jets without too much speed, or at a less acute angle.

TIPS

• Cross the eddy-line facing more across the current than usual.
• Don't hit the current hard enough to start planing unless it's narrow enough to plane right the way across.
• Change ends early and accelerate as you pass across the flow.
• Keep looking at the target eddy throughout the move.
• You may find that you land in the target eddy with more speed than you are used to.
• The timing of strokes and the transfer of edging are critical; to be too late with the transfer of edging will often result in a capsize. Rehearse it mentally before you actually do it.

S-cross Technique

1 Break into the current at about 45°, using your normal breaking-in technique.

2 Start paddling fast before you are facing downstream.

3 Charge forcefully across the current, and keep leaning the boat downstream as you do so.

4 Cross the opposite eddy-line. Aim to keep the boat moving at speed as it crosses the narrow current.

5 Change edges, using your legs, and begin the break-out sequence. This relies on excellent timing: practice is all.

6 You should finish the manoeuvre facing upstream in the other eddy.

Eddy Use and Etiquette

Now that we know the basics of getting into, out of and between eddies, it is time to learn a little about how they should be used. As has been explained, an eddy is an important river feature and the right etiquette and protocol should always be observed when using one.

Eddies are primarily used as a place to stop, rest and look ahead before running rapids. They vary in size; many are large enough for a whole group to stop and chat, whereas others might only be big enough for a single boat. Some people call very small eddies like this "micro eddies". In fact, they might be so tiny that only an expert paddler would ever notice them, let alone be able to land a boat in one in the middle of a powerful rapid.

This means that paddlers must think about the whole group when entering and leaving eddies. If an eddy fills up, one or more paddlers might have to carry

Entering a Micro Eddy

1 Attack the eddy-line more perpendicular than you would with a normal eddy.

2 Brake to reduce speed as you go across the eddy-line.

3 Level the boat early so that you don't spin back into the rapid.

4 Finish as close to the banks as you can without bouncing off the current.

◉ *A paddler in a large eddy and another approaching from upstream. This eddy is so big that etiquette isn't really an issue.*

on downstream without a plan. Before leaving an eddy, therefore, everyone should know where they are next going to eddy out – i.e. make their next stop.

Whoever is first into an eddy should back down or move away from the eddy-line so that the next paddler can also enter at the top. It is much better for everyone to break out as high up the eddy as they can; if someone misses they still have a chance to catch the eddy further down. The trouble is, sometimes this means that the person who was first into the eddy has to be the last out. This is one of the many reasons for having your best paddlers positioned first and last on the river.

In a very safe place where paddlers are playing on the rapid, it may not be necessary or appropriate to back away from the top of the eddy. Sometimes, other paddlers will be queuing to leave the top of the eddy, and it would be rude and unnecessary to jump to the front of the line. If you see that this is the case, join the back of the eddy queue like everyone else. If, on the other hand, you are anxious or out of control, aim for the top of the eddy – it is up to more experienced paddlers to recognize your problems and make room for you.

When you are ready to leave an eddy, make sure that there is no one paddling downstream who will end up too close to you, or who might be aiming for the part of the eddy that you are leaving. It is too easy on white water to miss what other people are trying to do, but being considerate is very important.

Eddy-hopping

It is important that a group of paddlers leaves an eddy knowing that they will be able to catch one another within the distance that they can see (or know from experience) is safe. This way of running a river from one eddy to the next is called "eddy hopping". However, it may not be possible for everyone to make the same eddy, so before you leave, look ahead and consider where you and everyone else in the group will break out next. In small eddies, it may be necessary for the paddlers to swap the lead.

An open canoe joins the top of an eddy. The kayakers have made room at the top to give him safer access.

Group dynamics in an eddy. The expert paddlers at the top and back of the eddy will leave first and last.

Running Rapids

Many rapids have hydraulic and/or rock features that can be hazardous, and you need to know how to avoid them, or deal with them if they are unavoidable.

Waves and Holes

The nature of hydraulics changes with the depth and flow of the water. Unbroken waves are usually no problem because you can paddle over them. If they get very big or are really close together, it may be sensible to take a diagonal route over them. However, a wave that is breaking hard can stop and hold the boat. In extreme cases, it will hurl the boat end over end, disorientating the paddler. You will learn from experience whether you're likely to punch through a wave or not.

As the depth reduces, the drop into the breaking pile becomes more pronounced, and the re-circulating water pours back into the depression. This hydraulic will hold the boat, and it is only safe if you can see that the ends are pointing downstream to allow you to escape.

● *This kayaker is on the towback of a powerful hydraulic, and the water is so aerated that his kayak barely floats. He must keep moving downstream to avoid being sucked back in.*

● *This rapid is full of big waves, although the water is too deep for them to form retentive "stoppers" or "holes", and the paddler's approach is dictated by comfort more than by safety.*

Reducing the depth of the water further turns this hole into a pourover. Pourovers are nearly always unpleasant because they do not allow the boater to ride comfortably on the front of the pile – there is too much water falling on the upstream side of the boat. Sometimes you can jump over the towback by paddling right through the pourover, but it is better to skirt around it.

Whenever you look at a hydraulic, try to imagine what will happen to the boat if you are held sideways in its grip. It takes experience to read the water in this way, and there is no better test than watching what someone else does. You will quickly learn to spot the little tongues of water that can provide a passage downstream, and to recognize whether the pile helps you towards an exit through which you can escape, or constantly pushes you away from it. Practise as much as you can by playing in holes that are small and safe, gradually moving on to more difficult ones. Once you can go into a hole, and come out again unscathed, you are well on the way to confidently running rapids.

🔺 *This is a particularly unpleasant scenario. A lot of water is falling steeply into a re-circulating stopper or hole. The white water is flowing back upstream from as far as 5m (16ft) downstream. A paddler or swimmer caught in this hydraulic would be swamped with water and would not be able to escape. In this example it is just about possible to sneak past the hole on either side, but the only sane route is on the bank.*

🔻 *Although this stopper has a big breaking foam pile, it is friendly because the drop into it is not too steep. It is very powerful and will hold the boat indefinitely, but a skilful paddler can remain in control and can effect an escape by simple paddling out of the end of the pile. The hole is safe because if you were to swim, you would be flushed downstream. This feature is called an elevated pile.*

Running Drops

If you want to try paddling over a drop of any significant size, you need to know what the water below is like. It is likely that you will not have a good view of the water from your boat. Vertical drops have different characteristics from sloping drops, but both present significant dangers to the paddler. They should always be inspected to check for rocks or trapped trees. On a vertical drop you can often measure the depth with a paddle.

Sloping Drops

A sloping drop will usually have a big hydraulic at the bottom that you may have to paddle through. Look for any gaps in the pile, or any sign of a downstream V. This will be the best spot. If the water going down the ramp is not flat but consists of two or more flows crossing over each other, you need to be on the top flow. The other(s) would carry you under the top one, and might flip your boat as it goes over the drop.

🔽 *This man is using a kayak paddle to check the depth of the pool below a small 1m (3½ft) waterfall. He can also make sure that there are no trees or other obstructions under the water that might entrap the submerged kayak when he runs the drop.*

🔼 *A kayaker is attempting a meltdown on a sloping drop where he had no chance of jumping the hydraulic.*

🔽 *Running a sloping drop into an eddy. The kayaker can take a diagonal line across this drop to get to the eddy.*

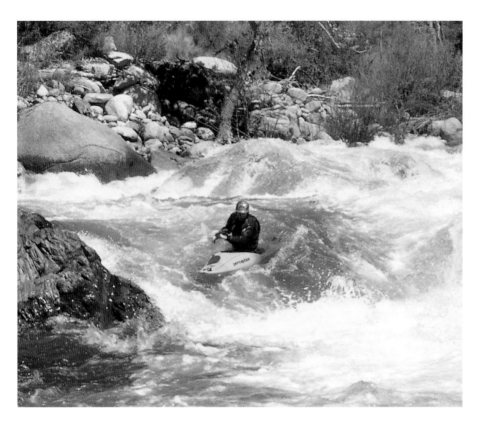

● *Running any kind of drop can be a serious undertaking and should not be attempted without careful thought. A huge white water rapid such as this is for experts only.*

Vertical Drops

Waterfalls usually have a deep and very strong hydraulic re-circulation system at the bottom, but you will usually land downstream of it. If the fall is so big that you cannot do this, consider the sanity of the undertaking. If going ahead, the main consideration is the height of the drop. Can you survive the impact uninjured, and is the water deep enough? Whatever the profile of the fall, there are basically two ways of running it.

Meltdown

A meltdown is a way of taking the drop so that your hull stays in contact with the green water all the way down, and you then go through, or under, the re-circulating hydraulic. It was invented by squirt boaters in the 1980s, and has revolutionized vertical drops in all but the most high-volume boats. Just paddle normally towards your chosen spot on the lip of the drop, keeping your weight forward. As you drop into the pile, tuck your head right forwards and down,

and put the paddle along the boat as if preparing for a roll. You may well need to roll, anyway, but the main reason for doing this is to prevent the pile from snapping the paddle across your chest.

If the drop is vertical, do not paddle too fast; drop over the edge at your current speed, or a little faster to retain some control. This will ensure you do not go out too far. Do not lean back as you see the water below because the boat may

over-rotate, and this may hurt. However, if the drop is sloping, the faster you are going when you hit the pile, the better your chance of sliding through. Just make sure the nose of the boat goes under the pile, not up the face of it.

Boof

A boof is the opposite way of taking a fall. This involves paddling hard off the lip of the drop, and keeping the weight back just before take-off, so that the boat shoots downstream a long way and lands flat on the hull. It helps if you make your last stroke right at the lip, and use your whole body to heave back the blade. This means that the boat is projected forwards, and your weight will be at the back as you start to fall. Throw yourself dynamically forward as soon as you are in freefall because this keeps the bow up, which helps the boat land flat and prevents the nose from plunging deep into the pile.

Boofing allows you to remain dry and in control, and you can land in shallow water if you get it right. Never boof high vertical drops unless the water below is very aerated, or you risk spinal compression. On a sloping drop, it is only possible to boof diagonally into an eddy – generally, you cannot get enough speed to clear the hydraulic unless it is a vertical fall.

● *Launching out from a waterfall in order to boof into the water below.*

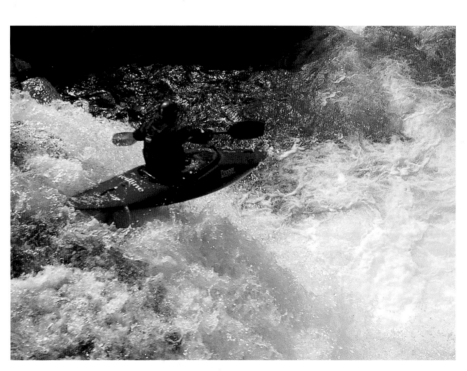

White Water Safety and Rescue

There are three main areas of risk that you need to protect yourself from while out on the water. Ultimately, the main threat is drowning, and you need to focus on the likely causes that can occur on white water.

Entrapment

The main killer of white water paddlers is entrapment. This can happen in rapids because they are typically fairly shallow, and filled with obstructions. The power of the water can easily pin a kayak against a rock, tree or even the river bed in such a way that you are powerless to dislodge it or escape from the boat. If you are trapped in this way with your head below the water, you will drown in a matter of seconds; rescuers do not have long to get you out and resuscitate you.

Fortunately, most people who venture on to white water are aware of this danger, while the relatively inexperienced will be strictly monitored by an instructor. There are many rapids on which you can practise where the danger of entrapment is minimal. As a general rule, note that entrapments are nasty and sudden, so take great care if you think there is the remotest chance of one happening.

◀ *If the bow of your kayak hits the bottom when negotiating a drop, you can get vertically pinned like this. The force of the water on your back makes it impossible to get out of the kayak. Sometimes you can shake the boat free or push off the bottom with your paddle, but the rule is, if you can breathe, don't move in case you make it worse. Rescuers can assist you by pulling the boat upwards to free the bow.*

The upstream side of any rock is a potential danger spot, where you can be pinned against an obstruction, often one that is submerged under the water level. Sometimes, if the water makes a cushion wave, you will not be trapped, but you cannot rely on that happening. A fallen tree or any object that has become embedded in the river bed can be a fatal hazard: avoid at all costs.

◔ *(Top) You can get into serious trouble if any part of your body becomes stuck between rocks on the river bed.*

◔ *(Above) If you hit the upstream side of a tree in moving water, this is how it can end. Even if you were on the surface when you hit the tree, the current will quickly force you below water level, and there is no escape. Avoid trees at all costs.*

If you do hit some type of obstruction and you get pinned against it, you must act quickly. There will be a brief moment of just a couple of seconds before things may start to take a turn for the worse. Throw your weight downstream towards the obstruction, and use every bit of your strength to lift the upstream edge of the boat before the water flows over you. With luck, you may then be able to drag

⬆ *This paddler has been swept into a rock in the middle of a rapid. By leaning on to the rock, he is holding the upstream edge of his boat above water, which saves him from disaster.*

yourself around the obstruction and release the boat from the pressure pinning it to the obstruction. If not, you are in trouble. If you can get right out of your boat and on to the rock or other obstruction, do it. These situations have a habit of deteriorating rapidly.

If you fail to hold the upstream rail up, the boat will angle down and become inextricably pinned. It may even start to fold up under the pressure of the water. You may be held in the boat by the force of the water, and might be unable to keep your head up. It is easy to say "Don't panic," but you have only got seconds to find a solution. Wriggle the boat around, and fight to get out. If you do get out, try to kick off in a direction that will take you around the obstruction and away.

Other entrapment dangers include vertical, shallow drops. It is possible to be rescued from this situation, but only if your fellow paddlers can get to you quickly, or are in position already,

⬆ *If the paddler can't lean downstream quickly enough, the current will flip the boat upstream and pin it in a position from which there may be no escape.*

⬆ *In this instance, things have gone wrong. The boat is pinned on the rock, but the paddler is able to get out and on to the rock to await rescue.*

⬆ *If a boat is pinned to a rock by the current, you need to mount a serious recovery operation from the shore, using ropes, to get the boat free.*

⬆ *Here, the paddler is using an elevated pull to lift the boat up from the rocks. The throw-line can then be used to drag the boat back to the shore.*

monitoring your progress. As a rule, a boat or person pinned to an obstacle by the current can only be released in the direction from which they came – usually upstream. If you cannot release the boat and have to extract the paddler, take care that the force of the water as he exits does not cause leg or other injuries.

Undercut rocks or cliffs are extremely dangerous. They are undercut because the current flows under them, and you can easily get trapped against the rocks. There may also be trees and other debris that has accumulated next to the rocks. If the water flows right up against a rock or bank, but there is not much of a cushion or pressure wave, assume that most of the current is flowing underneath the water surface: never paddle here.

Release and Recovery

If a boat is pinned by rocks, use one of the following pulls to dislodge it and/or drag it back to the shore.

A shoulder belay – in which the rope passes from the boat around your shoulders – is much more powerful than simply using your arms. The elevated pull is designed to lift the boat to reduce friction and water pressure while the boat is dragged away horizontally from the water. For the vector pull, tie a rope from the pinned boat to a tree or rock, then pull at 90° to the rope to reduce pressure on the boat and pull it free.

◐ *Using a vector pull to free a boat from entrapment on rocks in the water.*

Hydraulics

There are certain hydraulic wave features on white water that can stop and hold a kayak. In extreme cases, particularly on weirs and below waterfalls and pourovers, hydraulics are able to hold a swimmer and re-circulate him indefinitely. This is a potentially life-threatening situation.

The endless cycle of being submerged, surfacing, then being sucked upstream and submerged again rapidly leads to exhaustion. A swimmer in this situation can be rescued with a throw-line, or sometimes an experienced paddler can approach from downstream in a boat and pull him out. Self-extraction is extremely difficult, and impossible to practise safely. Prevention is always the best answer.

◐ *Wrapping the rope around your shoulders in a shoulder belay will make more effective use of your strength when recovering a boat from the water.*

White Water Swimming

Swimming down a rapid after a capsize has plenty of hazards besides the danger of entrapment. You are usually safer if you keep hold of your upturned boat because it will tow you through the hydraulics, and you can use it as a fender. If you have to make a choice between holding on to the paddle or the boat, choose the paddle: the boat will be easier to find later.

Position yourself so that you are upstream of the boat to avoid getting pinned. Face downstream and keep your legs up, pointing downstream, in what is known as the defensive swimming posture. You can use your feet to push yourself away from boulders, but be aware of the danger of getting your feet caught between rocks.

Keep holding on to your boat and paddle, and concentrate on conserving your energy. Wait for an opportunity to swim ashore, then head straight for the bank. If you still have the boat, ditch it if you are in any doubt about making it to safety. If you do not make it, the water will return you to the centre of the river and the attempt will have been wasted. You have limited reserves of energy, so choose your moment carefully.

◗ *A paddler caught in a hydraulic can be rescued with a throw-line from the shore, or by another paddler towing him to safety. However, the rescuer must be careful not to be sucked into the hydraulic himself.*

FOOT ENTRAPMENT

This is a very real threat. As soon as the foot is caught, the victim will fall down and the force of the current may hold him down and drown him. If you find your foot trapped, kick it upstream and upwards as hard as you can – yanking at it as you fall downstream will make things worse. To avoid foot entrapment, make it a rule never to stand in moving water more than 30cm (1ft) deep.

Using a Throw-line

A swimmer in the defensive posture can usually be rescued with a specialist rescue rope called a throw-line.

To rescue someone from the water, take your throw-line, open the bag and grasp the loose end of the rope. Throw the bag (NOT the rope) to the victim. Aim to land the bag beyond the swimmer, so that the rope falls across him, and he can grab it and be pulled to safety.

Throwing the bag and line can be tricky in fast moving water, particularly if the victim panics. All paddlers should practise throwing and catching the throw-line until they are confident they can use it.

◗ *The defensive swimming posture. Float with your feet up and facing downstream to avoid entrapment.*

◗ *When the time is right, turn on to your front and swim as hard as you can for the river bank.*

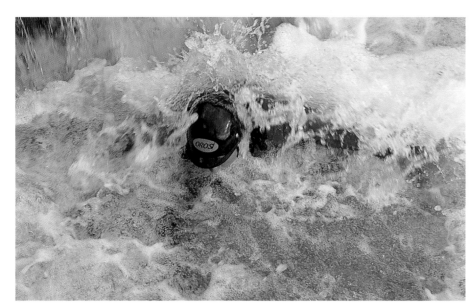

◗ *This man is trying to swim his way out of a powerful hydraulic after a capsize. Although the river is flowing from top to bottom in the picture, the man is being sucked back upstream by the re-circulating water and submerged again by the water pouring over the drop. The enormous force of the water means that with every attempt to move, the swimmer is becoming exhausted and less able to act decisively. If he can't find a way out of this re-circulating water (for example, by swimming to either end of the stopper or being pushed through by the main flow), this cycle will be repeated until he drowns or is rescued.*

OPEN HORIZONS

OPEN WATER AND SEA PADDLING

Kayaks and canoes are ideal for paddling over a great distance, or across exposed areas of open water. Indeed, both types of craft originated precisely because their builders needed to use them in this way, for hunting, trading and migration. The kayak is eminently suited to coastal and ocean travel, and the open canoe to exploring large rivers and great lakes.

The demands of long-distance paddling are quite special, and are unlike most of the other disciplines covered in this book. The main criterion is a need for speed because the distances covered can be quite long. Directional stability is equally important because one cannot paddle far in a boat that keeps veering away from straight lines. The boats also need to be very stable and easy to paddle. Long-distance boats need good storage space for food and water, and camping and survival equipment.

◀ *Riding an ocean wave. Surfing is now a hugely popular branch of paddle sport.*

�),*Two paddlers in modern traditionally-styled sea kayaks explore a rocky coastline.*

Tides and Currents

Knowing about tides and currents is extremely important if you are planning to paddle a boat out at sea or on any large body of water. Ignoring them means possibly endangering your safety.

Tides

The tide is a familiar concept to anyone living or working near the sea, but it can be exceptionally confusing to others. All over the world, the sea and other large bodies of water are visibly moved by the gravitational effect of the moon, and to a lesser extent by the sun and planets. With only a few exceptions, this results in the water rising and falling twice a day – in any 24-hour period there will be two high tides and two low tides, with the water rising and falling fairly predictably from one to the next.

The size of the variation depends on two things: where you are in the world, and the date. Every month there is a cycle of tidal variation, which sees more extreme tides (highest highs and lowest lows) around the time of the full moon and 14 days later, reducing to less extreme ones (with a smaller change in height from highs to lows) in the weeks

in between. The extreme tides are known as spring tides, and the moderate tides are known as neap tides.

There is also a yearly variation. The biggest spring tides will be those that occur worldwide around the time of the equinoxes (when the sun crosses the equator) on 21 March and 21 September, and the smallest around the solstices (when the sun is furthest from the equator) on 21 June and 21 December.

It is useful to understand how tidal variations occur but there is no substitute for getting a tide table or checking the time of high and low tide on the day you

◔ A sheltered estuary at high tide. Always remember that the tide comes in and out twice a day, with currents much faster than you can paddle.

plan to paddle. If there is no appropriate information service available in the area, look for the information on the internet. Tides can vary by up to an hour between places only 100km (60 miles) apart.

◔ The same estuary as above, shown here at low tide. As well as the currents, you will have to contend with difficult access over deep mud banks.

◔ The high-tide level of this river is clearly visible. At low tide there is access to the grassy bank, but at high tide there is no accessible landing spot.

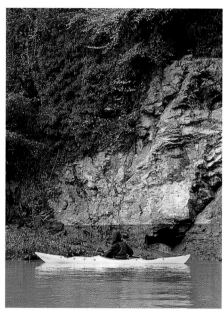

Currents

Although we describe the tide as rising and falling, there is a dramatic flow of water associated with it in many areas. The sea can exhibit strong tidal currents that are, in many cases, faster flowing than a river's. This is dangerous because you could set off when the water is slack at high or low tide, and find yourself a few hours later in a raging torrent like Skookumchuck in British Columbia, Canada, the Bitches in Wales or the Falls of Lora in Scotland, a situation for which you might be totally unprepared.

In most cases, the effects of a sea current are much the same as on a river. Good paddling technique will help you deal with the possible eddies and waves. There is, however, a special type of current called a rip that can be found in coastal areas. This can be dangerous to swimmers, but is a mixed blessing to paddlers who can use it to their advantage, as long as they know how.

The rip is a current most often found on surf beaches. The ocean swells breaking on the shore push a lot of water onshore, and this water has to run back

The directional pull of the current. A rip takes water out to sea, while the longshore drift moves around the land.

into the sea. Usually, it flows back in one or two spots, dictated by the shoreline, creating currents flowing back out through the waves. Anything in the area will be drawn towards the rip, and towed out to sea through the surf. You can see where they are from a cliff top, because the waves look flatter, but they are almost impossible to see at sea level. If you want to get out through the waves, a rip can

This exposed beach could be prone to strong currents. Find out about local currents before launching out to sea.

offer a welcome free ride. If you are in trouble or are trying to stay inshore, you must get out of the rip by paddling or swimming straight across it to water that is going inshore. Never try to fight against it, which is exhausting and futile.

Longshore drift

Rip tide

Rip tide

Rip tide

Wind and Waves

When paddling on the open sea, winds and waves are important features, and they can have an immediate effect on what you are trying to do. It is crucial that you appreciate their power, and the way in which they work.

Wind Types

It does not take a strong wind to affect a boat. Even a light breeze, which you would barely notice on shore, can have quite a dramatic effect. Surprisingly, it is not paddling into the wind that causes most people problems, because this merely slows you down. A following wind is the one to look out for.

When it strikes, your boat will constantly try to turn around to face upwind, and most of your energy is used to keep the boat pointing the way you want to go. Kayaks suffer the worse from this; canoes a little less so, especially if a solo paddler is sitting in the back. It happens because the centre of drag of the boat (the deepest part of it, where most of your weight is) is usually quite far forward, and the tail half of the boat slews around quite easily. Boats are often designed this way to make them easy to

 The wind has a huge effect on waves, which should never be underestimated.

turn. The solution is to have a skeg, or rudder, at the back, or even to move your weight back if you can, to make the tail a little heavier. Some short boats as short as 3m (10ft) long, are very difficult to paddle in a following wind.

A cross-wind has much the same effect, blowing the tail away and making the boat turn towards the wind. It is less annoying and more predictable than a tail-wind because you know which way it wants to turn, but it is still very tiring as you constantly have to sweep stroke to

keep the boat on track. Many of the design features of sea kayaks are specifically intended to combat the effect of wind, but they can never eradicate it completely without rendering the boat impossible to manoeuvre.

When planning your trip, get accurate weather forecasts to see what conditions are likely, and remember that wind directions can change very suddenly. In warm weather, there is a tendency for winds to blow offshore at night as the land cools and the air over it flows out to sea. As the temperature rises through the day, the wind blows increasingly strongly onshore towards the warmer land. It is possible to experience winds swinging a full 360° in one 24-hour period. Mariners refer to a wind blowing onshore as lee shore conditions; an offshore wind creates a weather shore.

Waves

On the open sea, waves are caused by the wind unless the water is moving quickly over submerged rocks. In the latter case, the effect is exactly the same as a white water river. Wind-blown waves are another matter, and they fall into two categories: chop and swell.

Waves without wind. This shore is catching a big ocean swell, but there may still be places to launch and land.

● *Onshore wind. Wind on its own isn't a danger, but the effect it has on the swell makes for heavy surf conditions.*

Chop

Random small waves, created by variable winds over a short distance, are known as chop. A calm sea can become choppy in a matter of minutes when the wind strength increases. Chop can be confusing for paddlers because waves seem to come at them from all directions. The best thing is to ignore the waves as much as possible – try to relax and trust your balance. Sometimes it can help to surf the waves, if only for a few seconds.

Swell

Winds blowing in the same direction for a long distance create a swell. The longer the wind pushes, the bigger the waves get. Winds blowing around the outside of a storm system commonly send 6m (20ft) waves radiating out across the ocean. Once these waves are made, they do not diminish unless they meet an oncoming wind, which reduces them. They will still be very large even after travelling 1,000km (620 miles) without any further power from the wind that created them.

Swell only ever occurs over oceanic distances, and is rarely a concern in small enclosed seas such as the Mediterranean.

Small swells of 1m (3½ft) can occur, for example, in some of the larger lakes in the North American and Canadian Great Lakes, but they do not rival the swells of the Pacific or Atlantic, which commonly reach 10m (33ft) high.

When paddling in the sea, you could experience chop and swell at the same time, and in fact this is very common. If you can think of the two as separate features, superimposed on each other and to be treated independently, you will not find them difficult to deal with.

Wind with Waves

A combination of wind and waves can occur in a variety of ways. Since choppy water is always associated with a local wind, you will have the latter to contend with as well. When the conditions become severe, with a 1m (3½ft) chop, you might find yourself in a trough, but when you go over a wave you will be hit by a savage gust that might even capsize you. Be ready for this. Anticipate, and lean into the wind, keeping your paddles low to stop the wind catching them.

Swells are affected by the wind direction. A following wind (onshore) will blow the tops off the waves and make them crumble rather than pitch. Offshore winds will steepen the faces of the waves, and make them rear up and crash down as they break.

One of the most notable effects of winds, waves and currents is the difference between wind blowing in the same direction as the tide and wind against the tide. If the tide creates a current flowing strongly downwind, the water might be smooth despite quite windy conditions. When the tide turns and the water is flowing against the wind, there might be a dramatic worsening of the conditions at sea until the area resembles a rapid, with large standing waves as well as chop.

● *The effects of swell and wind-chop superimposed on one another.*

Navigation and Distance

It is easy to think of touring and sea paddling as placid activities, far removed from the demands of white water, but a river flows in only one direction, and this makes it hard to get lost. On the sea there is a far greater chance of ending up in the wrong place, and the demands on your physical strength and stamina mean that you will tire more easily. No matter how confident a paddler you are inland, at sea you need to be able to navigate and chart your position, and accurately gauge how far you and your group can paddle without tiring.

Navigational Equipment

Different types of open water paddling call for different pieces of navigational equipment, but you should always take a compass with you whenever you paddle on the sea, on large lakes or on estuaries. The most important point with any equipment is that you know how to use it correctly, otherwise it will be useless.

⊙ *Maps can be laminated to make them waterproof. Some spraydecks (skirts) have an accessory to hold maps in place.*

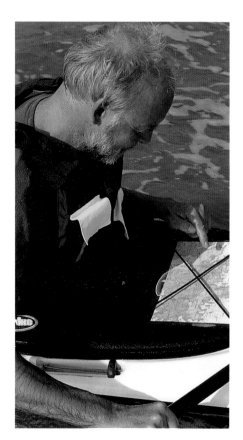

Compass, Charts and Maps

If you are planning to spend the duration of your trip within easy reach of the shore, there is little need for sophisticated navigational equipment, but whenever you paddle on large lakes, rivers and the sea you should always have a compass with you, just in case. You also need to be sure that you know how to use the compass properly. At sea, a chart is extra insurance and will help you to identify onshore landmarks.

If you intend to make a significant open-water crossing, you must study basic nautical navigation. It is important that you can decide what compass bearing to paddle on to reach your goal, and that you can pay attention to it during your trip. It is rarely a case of pointing your boat where you want to go – at best this usually results in paddling much further than necessary, and at worst you might never get there.

If you are at sea and a fog descends unexpectedly (as it so often can do), a compass and a good knowledge of your locale make the difference between getting ashore safely and needing to be rescued by the emergency services. Paddling in the dark is great fun, and navigation at night can often be easier than by day if you can identify the onshore lights. Even so, you still need to be equipped with a compass.

Global Positioning System

For adventurous paddlers planning longer trips out at sea, more sophisticated navigational equipment is now available. The high-tech gadget known as the global positioning system (GPS) will provide you with a definitive position (a grid reference), and indicate which way you are travelling and how fast, which is invaluable information when the land is out of sight. The GPS is now becoming increasingly popular and affordable. If you can afford one, and want to use the very best navigational technology, it is a brilliant acquisition, although you will need a chart and a compass to use with it. Make sure you know how to use it correctly before you set out to sea.

⊙ *A compass mounted securely on the front deck hatch of a sea kayak. This is invaluable equipment for open water.*

Lighting

Not only is it important that you can identify your location with accuracy on open water, you also need to be well lit yourself. If you ever need the help of a rescue crew, they won't be able to find you unless you are visible. There is also a very real chance that you could be hit by a larger boat that cannot see your tiny craft. Always find out in advance what kind of shipping uses the water you are planning to paddle on, and plan the route of your trip accordingly.

Even if you are planning to paddle only 1km (½ mile) offshore, you need to make sure you can be seen clearly. Many paddlers use chemical glow-stickers attached to their boats and their helmets and clothing to make them visible at night. Glow-stickers do not ruin your night vision, and they have the advantage of needing no batteries or precautions against soaking. They are available from most boating suppliers and some large DIY stores.

It always pays to be prepared for all eventualities, just in case you ever do need to take evasive action. If paddling out at sea, include a strobe light and flares as part of your safety and rescue equipment. For emergency use – for example, if you think a larger boat may collide with you – a strobe light is extremely bright and eye-catching, and your best chance of attracting attention. If you do not have a strobe, use a flare.

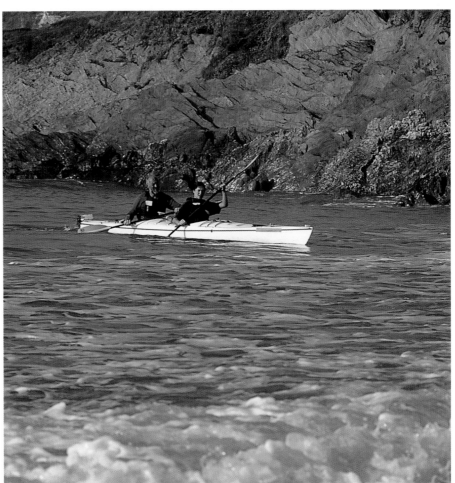

● *Younger children can paddle in double boats with an adult; they should always wear a flotation aid.*

● *Your personal limits can vary. If you feel less than 100 per cent on the day, your stamina will be affected.*

Know your Limits

It is important to know how far you and the rest of your group can paddle before tackling the open water. Bear in mind that your range on sheltered flat water will be greater than out at sea, where conditions are more demanding: paddling against a wind or current can make a big difference to your range, as can the roughness of the sea. Your response and strength can only be learnt from experience, so don't present yourself with too much of a challenge to begin with.

Children can run out of energy quite suddenly; when they do, they may refuse to co-operate, and towing them will be essential. The best solution is to have them in a double boat with an adult. This way they will not tire as quickly because the adult will do most of the paddling.

OPEN WATER EQUIPMENT

Open water, sea and long-distance paddling has special demands, and the boats usually differ dramatically from those used for inland day boating. There is also a variety of other accessories that can make touring in a kayak or canoe that much safer and more enjoyable. The key issue is self-sufficiency.

If you are likely to be away from any possible assistance for much of your journey, you will have to carry everything with you. You might end up using a fully equipped, expedition sea kayak. If, on the other hand, you are going to be a short distance from populated areas for the whole journey, your only considerations are comfort, and a credit card may be all you need.

Finally, it is important that you have everything you need to be safe and comfortable, but equally important that you can carry your boat. Do not attempt to take every gadget that could possibly come in handy. The emphasis should be on keeping it light. If you cannot carry the boat, how well can you paddle it?

Paddling on the open sea is awesome, but make sure you are sufficiently equipped.

Open water gear can be stowed on the boat in waterproof compartments.

Boats for Open Water

The range of open-water boats available can be divided into sea or inland, and kayak or canoe. Many of the key issues that need to be accommodated for by the boats' design are the same, whether it is a kayak or a canoe, to be used on inland waterways or the ocean. There are a variety of first-rate boats that can be used for both touring and open and sea-water paddling, and these will give you maximum flexibility.

Kayaks

Sea kayaks are intended for coastal and open-sea touring, but they can be used for touring inland and can negotiate simple rapids up to Grade (Class) 2 as easily as ocean waves. There are also light, fast, narrow sea boats suitable for day trips, and bigger, heavier ones aimed at trips and expeditions lasting several days. Both have waterproof bulkheads and hatches to contain essential equipment. They can be used with or without a rudder; purist paddlers object to

◆ *An open canoe is an ideal platform for exploring marinas such as this.*

rudders because they think the kayaker should be able to control the boat without one, but do not let that put you off. Some boats have small, traditional cockpits, and others modern keyhole ones.

Double kayaks can be a faster and more sociable way to travel. Some have provision for carrying children in their mid-section. They have most of the features found in solo kayaks, but will also have a rudder because the boats are too long to manoeuvre without one.

◆ *Open boats are a popular choice for one or more paddlers taking excursions on inland lakes and waterways.*

Touring kayaks are usually less comprehensively equipped than the sea boats, but often have many of the same features. The hull design tends to be the main difference, the emphasis being on manageability in more restricted conditions on inland water rather than sea-worthiness in extreme conditions.

⊙ *Modern touring kayaks suitable for inland, coastal or open sea use.*

Canoes

Except for those canoes used on challenging stretches of white water, canoes tend to have fewer fittings and features than their counterpart kayaks. This belies the fact that subtleties of hull design can make a huge difference to the way the canoe behaves.

Touring canoes are built to cope with tracking and windage, which is the deflection of the boat off its route by the wind. They have a significant keel, and more balanced seating positions than other kinds of canoe. However, there is less specific provision for storage in a canoe than a kayak, despite its greater load-carrying capability.

Some canoe models have air tanks for flotation. These are usually small, forming seats in the bow and stern. They can be used for additional storage, and are reached through a waterproof hatch. However, they are not very common in touring boats, the very boats in which you might want to carry bulky camping or other equipment. Usually you will have to store gear in large dry bags or drums, which can be lashed to the seats to keep them securely in place.

Touring canoes are sometimes used for coastal paddling, but you should rarely venture far away from the shore in one because they are much more susceptible to the wind than sea kayaks, making them less easy to control. However, they do have one advantage: even if you cannot roll a touring canoe you can still right it, re-enter it, and bail out in the event of a capsize. For a full description of this method of self-rescue, see the technique, *Right Boat and Re-enter.*

⊙ *Paddling a sea/touring kayak. Note the waterproof hatches and the deck lines for attaching gear, safety and rescue equipment and spare paddles.*

Deck Fittings

Touring kayaks usually have deck lines, which are ropes running along and across the deck for handling the boat, and under which you can store equipment. Some of the cross-lines might be made from shock cord for securing a map or other item.

Canoes, clearly, do not have a deck on which to stow things but, if you need to lash down a lot of gear, a good solution is a cargo net, which can also be used for tying or hooking on quick-access items.

Pumps

Inevitably, you will ship water if paddling for a long time. A hand pump can be used to bail out a kayak or canoe. Some kayaks come equipped with hand pump and/or foot pumps, which means you can pump out water with your spraydeck still attached. As a rule, hand pumps move more water, but you need one or both hands free to operate them. The foot pump is a slower way to get the water out, but at least you can carry on using your paddle, which might be essential in rough seas. When choosing a pump, think about what you are likely to face in your paddling. After a capsize and re-entry (canoe or kayak), you will definitely have to pump out water, but this is an extreme case. If you're not going to be doing anything like this, the money might be better spent on a really good spraydeck to keep the water out, and a sponge for the annoying splashes you ship while getting in and out.

Paddles for Open Water

There is a wide choice of paddles for use on open water and the sea, from wing to split kinds. Paddles for touring and open water need different design features to paddles for general-purpose flat and white water paddling. Here we look at some of the popular advanced styles of touring paddles.

The most important issue when deciding which kind of paddle to buy is weight. If you are going to paddle for a long time, you need blades which are as light as possible. This means that modern high-tech composite materials are most people's first choice, but many paddlers still like wooden paddles, too.

Long paddles are also important to achieve a low paddling angle. This is especially true for kayaking, but even touring canoeists tend to use longer paddles with narrower blades.

Whatever paddle you choose, inspect it carefully before each use, and remember that your ability to move the boat, steer and roll relies on the integrity of your paddle. A damaged blade might break off just when you need it most.

● *Symmetrical bladed paddles work very well for touring and open water.*

Symmetrical Blades

The simple, symmetrical paddle is perfectly adequate for touring despite the undoubted benefits of more specialized designs. Make sure that your symmetrical blade is curved and spooned, or has a dihedral face, or it will flutter and will be difficult to paddle with over any distance.

Asymmetrical Blades

Paddle blades with an asymmetrical edge are more efficient than the equivalent symmetrical kind, and they make less splash in the water. The reasons for this

● *Asymmetical blades are less splashy and more efficient for forward paddling.*

● *A replica of a traditional Greenland paddle, as used by Inuit paddlers. It is so narrow that it gives little support, but it propels the kayak well.*

are clear when you look at how a paddle blade enters the water for a stroke. The disadvantage is that you must pick it up the right way round to get the full benefit.

Paddle Shafts

One notable feature of open water paddles is the shaft design. Many touring paddlers use bent paddle shafts. Kayak paddles are available with ergonomically curved shafts, which are very helpful in preventing some of the repetitive strain injuries that long-distance kayaking can cause. Canoe paddles are also available with these ergo shafts, or with a simpler

● *The bent paddle shaft is less likely to strain the wrists over long distances.*

Spare and Split Paddles

If you are planning to paddle a long distance, or a long way from the shore, you might want to take spare paddles with you in case any member of the group loses or damages their paddle. In a canoe it is easy to store a spare paddle under the seat, but this is a little more difficult in a kayak. The usual solution is to have a set of split (break-down) paddles that can be secured under the deck lines of your kayak, so that they do not get in the way of your paddling. By storing them here, it is possible to access them to roll with half a paddle if you lose your main paddle when knocked flat by a wave.

Spraydecks for Touring

These spraydecks (spray skirts) are not necessarily different to those worn for flat or white water, but few paddlers want to have a tight neoprene tube around their waist when paddling over a long distance and for several hours. Some paddlers choose to wear nylon spraydecks to avoid this, but these will let in water and allow water pools to form on the deck. A good solution is a combination touring deck. This comprises a neoprene deck with a fabric body tube, and will sometimes have braces to hold it up. With this deck you will have the advantages of both systems.

Though it is rare to break a paddle, the consequences can be dire if you are a long way from the shore. Split (break-down) paddles are carried on deck or stowed in the boat as insurance in case this happens.

bend, so that the blade is at an angle to a normal, straight paddle shaft. The latter simply allows the blade of the paddle to address the water at a more efficient angle, rather than altering the ergonomics of your physical movement.

Wing Paddle

The wing paddle was invented for kayak racing, but many of its benefits make it useful for touring. The wing paddle is supremely efficient and it helps to stabilize the boat. The blade moves through the water in an arc, which

utilizes many more muscle groups than does a conventional paddle, thereby making each stroke far more powerful.

Greenland Paddle

The Greenland paddling technique is described in *Stroke Variations*. The actual Greenland paddle acquired its long thin shape because the Inuit peoples who designed it did not have the right materials to make wider, flatter blades. There are some advantages to the design, such as low windage (deflection caused by the wind), and the fact that you can use the paddle as a club, or can wind your fishing tackle around it, although these are dubious benefits for today's kayaker. Those who use this paddle do so because they enjoy using traditional equipment and mastering the same challenges as the Inuit.

This touring spraydeck features a neoprene deck with a fabric body tube and represents the best of both worlds for long-distance paddling.

Open Water Clothing and Accessories

It is vital that you make the right choices with clothing for open water and the sea, not least so that you feel comfortable and warm. There is a wide choice of clothing available, and newcomers might feel slightly bewildered, but these guidelines will point you in the right direction.

Clothing for open- and sea-water paddling varies much more than that for white water because the emphasis is on versatility, due to the changing nature of the conditions. It is quite usual to take a choice of clothing with you in the boat.

Insulation

Though this is usually the same as for any other active sport, it is vital that you have a number of layers so that you can adjust your insulation level to suit the changing conditions. If you stop paddling you will notice a dramatic drop in your perceived temperature, unless you use a combination of fairly expensive layers.

Breathable Shells

It is usually necessary to have a wind- and waterproof shell garment with you, even if you do not wear it all the time. This should always be made from a breathable fabric that allows the vapour from perspiration to

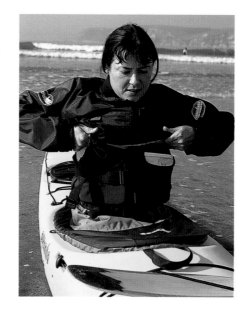

◉ *A cagoule may not be necessary in fine weather but it is useful to have one with you if you become chilly.*

escape, otherwise it will condense and you will become increasingly cold and wet. Some paddlers prefer a shell that they can put on over a buoyancy aid (personal flotation device) while they are afloat. Be aware, though, that capsizing with a cagoule over your head

◉ *You may want to remove your cagoule, but you should always keep on the flotation device.*

can be a frightening experience: it would be very difficult to free yourself or to remove your spraydeck if you became tangled up in your garment underwater! In fine weather, a cagoule may be unnecessary, but it is very useful to be able to put one over your buoyancy aid if your thighs turn chilly. No matter how warm the weather, it is absolutely essential that you wear your buoyancy aid when paddling on the sea.

There are jackets and cagoules specially designed for paddlers. They are much better, and cheaper, than using a breathable walking jacket, which would fall apart very quickly if used for boating. In more extreme sea paddling conditions some kayakers wear cagoules. These are not quite as good as dry tops, but they have the advantage that they offer a little more adjustability and ventilation. They usually come with a hood, and are modern versions of the Inuit tuvilik or paddling jacket, which was made from sealskin. In Arctic and sub-Arctic conditions it is necessary to wear survival or drysuits because of the extremely short survival time should a paddler fall into the water.

▶ *A good-quality kayaking jacket for use on open water and the sea.*

Trousers

Many open water paddlers prefer
salopettes, which are trousers with braces
attached to hold them up, because they
are more versatile, and provide a bit of
upper body protection when worn without
a jacket. Basic over-trousers are also
popular, and these will keep the wind out
when you are not in the boat. The choice
of lower body wear for kayaking depends
on how much time you will spend on land:
whereas the canoeist will have his or her
lower body exposed to the elements
the whole time, the kayaker is relatively
protected from the elements and has little
need of extra insulation when paddling.
Wetsuits are not appropriate for this
type of paddling because they are fairly
restrictive, can become hot and clingy,
and are generally too uncomfortable to
be worn for long periods.

*Durable polyethylene containers,
known as BDHs, are ideal for storing
small items that need to be kept dry.*

*A roll-top dry
bag is useful for
carrying items
such as mobile
phones and
car keys.*

Headgear

It is unusual to wear a helmet while
touring, but you may need to keep your
head warm. It is well known that most of
your body's heat loss is from the head so,
if you are getting cold, wear a hood or a
hat. Any hat will do; a woollen hat is a
popular choice because it is very warm,
but it can get heavy when wet.
In sunny conditions a hat with
a peak or brim is invaluable.
If your hat does not stay
firmly on your head,
you might want to tie it
on, or attach it to your
collar; if you don't, it is
likely to blow away in a strong gust of
wind. Of course, in colder weather you
may be wearing a paddling shell with a
hood, and this can serve the same
purpose as a hat, without the likelihood of
it falling off and blowing away.

*Two sea kayakers appropriately
dressed for the conditions. Despite the
sunshine, sharp sea winds mean that
warm headgear may still be needed.*

Additional Gear

Many items such as mobile phones, car
keys and first aid kits need to be kept dry.
The dry compartments of a sea kayak are
not 100 per cent waterproof and, in any
case, it is better to have really important
items on your person.

Dry bags are a good way to protect
your essentials from the water. There are
different types, but the most common is
the roll-top variety. For dryness and more
protection, use screw-top polyethylene
jars, known as BDH containers after the
chemical company that invented them.
These are available from paddling stores.
They are only 100 per cent waterproof
if used with a rubber seal inside the lid.

Safety and Rescue Equipment

You can meet all kinds of problems, from being injured and requiring a tow back ashore to attracting sharks drawn by your flailing legs as you attempt to swim for safety. The following equipment should help to guarantee your safety.

Flotation

The buoyancy aid (personal flotation device or PFD) should be worn at all times when paddling on open water or the sea. Styles of buoyancy aid vary but the emphasis for most sea and touring paddlers seems to be on having pockets in which you can carry certain essential items. Apart from this, the important thing is comfort. You will see many touring paddlers wearing a buoyancy aid that is incorrectly adjusted or unzipped, simply because it is not designed for long-term comfort. If they were to capsize, they would have difficulty doing up the buoyancy aid in the water, and would

◉ *A typical buoyancy aid (personal flotation device) for sea paddling. It has bright panels and retro-reflective tape for visibility, and a selection of pockets for survival essentials.*

experience all kinds of problems through not being able to keep hold of the boat and paddles.

Many buoyancy aids have some retro-reflective material, making them and the wearer more visible in poor light. This safety feature is not so visible when you are swimming though, in which case consider retro-reflective cuffs on your jacket, or a strobe light.

Whistle

A whistle is very useful if you need to attract attention in open water. Sound carries a long way over open water, and it could be that it is the only way to alert rescuers to your position.

Strobes and Beacons

A specialist strobe light is essential for anyone going offshore. When switched on it will flash at a rate that is quickly recognized by the rescue services, and be visible over a long distance. If attached to the shoulder of a buoyancy aid it will be seen even when you are swimming. Some offshore paddlers also take radio or satellite

◉ *Additional items for a sea trip might include a hand pump, knife, compass, VHF radio, transistor receiver, sunscreen and a mobile phone.*

beacons with them. When activated they send out a signal that is detected by special receivers, or even satellites, which alert the emergency services, giving them your exact position. The disadvantage is that they can be accidentally activated.

Flares

Flares are a common piece of safety kit to ensure that you can attract attention in case of an emergency. They can be

◉ *Many types of flares are available commercially; these flares are a popular choice for offshore paddling.*

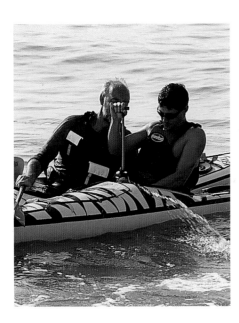

The most important point about towing is to ensure that you can release the tow, using the quick release buckle, if you get into difficulties yourself.

Bivvy Bag

This is possibly the best piece of safety kit ever made. If you have nothing else, an orange plastic bivvy bag can be a lifesaver. It is light, takes up little space, and can be used in four ways:

• To keep a victim warm when back on land: put them in the bag and, in extreme cases, get in with them to add your own body heat and increase their temperature.

• To keep yourself alive in the water. If you get into a bivvy in the water, it dramatically reduces the rate at which you lose heat. You can extend your cold-water survival time tenfold because while your body will heat up the water around you, you will keep the warm water in the bag, rather than constantly exchanging it for more cold water. You may also be less likely to get unwanted attention from predators such as sharks, because you will be big and orange and wafting gently rather than small, flailing and behaving like an injured seal.

• To attract attention by waving it around.

• To build a shelter from the sun, wind or rain when stranded ashore.

A waterproof first-aid kit suitable for all kinds of outdoor activities, including paddling. The orange plastic bivvy bag (right) is invaluable.

◉ *Using a waist-towline to recover a kayak after a capsize.*

◉ *The towline packs away neatly into a pouch worn as a belt.*

◉ *Pumping water out of a sea kayak using a hand pump. Excess water in the boat can be a real discomfort.*

spotted over greater distances than a strobe, and without many of the problems of radio beacons. You will need to carry a minimum of three flares. Always check that your flares are within their "use-by" date, otherwise they may not work.

Towline

A towline is a useful piece of equipment for helping other paddlers. You might need to tow a boat back to a swimmer, an injured or tired paddler ashore, or help a slower one keep up. The line is usually worn around the waist, but some paddlers have towing systems built into the deck of their kayak.

A simple tow can be attached to the front of the boat you are helping. If more paddlers are on hand to help, it is worth considering a husky tow, which means that two or more paddlers pull.

OPEN WATER PADDLING SKILLS

People who only paddle canoes and kayaks on flat or open water often pay less attention to the basic paddling skills than those involved in white water or other specialist disciplines. This is understandable because they think that precise manoeuvring skills and technical strokes are wasted on flat water, or water with a lot of room to move around on. What these paddlers do not understand is that the better and more efficiently you can paddle, the farther and faster you will go on flat and sea water with the same amount of effort.

If you take up open water paddling or touring, having reached a level of proficiency in a general-purpose boat, you may well find that you have to modify your approach. In a short, simple kayak, many strokes are even more effective if done aggressively and explosively. But in a longer touring kayak, or when countering the effect of the wind, you may need more finesse and subtler leans to make the stroke work, and this can be very satisfying. The same applies to canoes – perhaps even more so. That is why it is so important that you respond sensitively to your boat and your paddle.

❮ Setting out to sea in a boat gives an overwhelming sense of freedom.

❯ Sea kayaks offer plenty of opportunity for camping and touring trips.

Stroke Variations

When paddling long distances in touring boats, or in the windy conditions often found on open water, you will need to adopt a different paddling style and in some cases learn new techniques.

Slide Hand

As we have already mentioned, kayak paddles for touring tend to be longer than a general-purpose or white water paddle. This is partly so that you can paddle with a lower stroke, reducing the effect of the wind, the chance of being blown off course or being capsized. A high paddle stroke is more efficient in still air, but a low stroke can be essential in a breeze, and is certainly more relaxing if you are paddling a long way.

One excellent low-stroke technique, called the Greenland slide hand, originated with the Inuit people of Greenland. They recognized the benefits of a narrow blade and a small overall paddle size in a strong wind. The technique involves holding the paddle with one hand, close to the middle, and the other near, or holding, the blade. You can then make a stroke with an extended reach, which allows a lower paddle angle, as well as more leverage to keep a wayward boat on track.

As the paddle goes across to make a stroke on the other side, slide the hands to use the same grip at the other end of the paddle. The action is almost one of throwing the paddle across, and catching it in the required grip just as the stroke begins. The technique can be used

continuously while paddling forward, or just to increase your reach in order to turn difficult boats more easily.

The picture below shows a paddler using a traditional Greenland paddle, but the technique can be used with any kayak paddle that does not have a bent shaft.

Assisted Turns

Another way to make a touring boat turn more easily is by using a dramatic outside lean. Whether moving forward or stationary, most straight-running boats, which have a long keel to assist tracking, will be much easier to turn if you lean them over to reduce the effect of the keel. Leaning to the inside or the outside might work, but an outside lean is better when going forward because you can then lean on your sweep stroke which, with an extended grip, can be very supportive indeed.

Sculling for Support

The concept of using a blade in a sculling action was described in the basic kayak and canoe paddling skills chapter. Sculling for support was deliberately

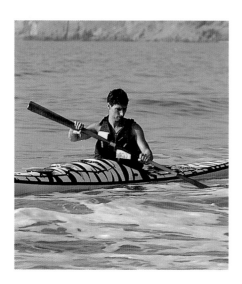

🔵 *Using a slide hand for forward paddling with a Greenland paddle. The top hand is holding the paddle at the blade. As the stroke ends, the paddle is slid across to be held at the other end. It feels odd but works surprisingly well.*

🔵 *Sculling for support is a skill that can prove very useful in a long, narrow closed cockpit kayak.*

omitted because it is a more advanced skill and much more difficult to achieve. In most general-purpose kayaks sculling for support is ineffective, and it is best avoided altogether in canoes. In a long, narrow boat such as a sea kayak, however, it can be very useful.

The sculling support stroke can help the paddler to avoid a capsize. It uses essentially the same action as the sculling draw, but the paddle blade is placed face down on the water. If the boat is at a dramatic lean angle, sculling can support it there indefinitely, whereas a low or high brace would only provide lift for long enough to recover to an upright position. An expert can scull with the boat laid completely on its side, provided his body is in the water and effectively supporting itself.

Many people find it easier to lie back while sculling for support, and this is recommended by many older books and instructors. However, it is safer and more effective to maximize your reach by remaining perpendicular, particularly once your body is immersed. The danger of lying back while sculling or high bracing is that it strains the shoulder, which can lead to injury, and the position makes it difficult to control the boat.

◉ *Sliding the hands to one end enables the paddler to lean over for much of the stroke, which helps the boat to turn.*

Knifed-J and Figure Eight

These two strokes are peculiar to open canoeing, and though fairly obscure, they are worth mentioning because they are useful in windy conditions. Sometimes, particularly when paddling solo in a single-seater boat, it seems that every time you take your blade out of the water the boat blows off line. The solution is not to take it out at the end of the stroke, but to turn it flat to the hull and slice it forward to where the stroke started. In its simplest form this is called a knifed-J. The blade rotates at the end of the stroke and is ready to knife forward through the water, controlling the tracking without slowing down the boat.

A more complex version is the figure eight. It is a powerful stroke for controlling inside turns and is sometimes called an Indian stroke. It is similar to the knifed-J stroke, except that after the blade slices forward the T-grip is rotated in the palm of the top hand so that the next stroke is made with what was the back of the paddle. The figure eight is only suitable for fairly flat paddles.

Both the knifed-J and the figure eight are also very useful for sneaking up on wildlife, when taking the blade out of the water would make audible splashing and dripping sounds.

Re-entry and Roll

If you are paddling a sea or touring kayak on open water, this is a skill that will give you great confidence. If conditions are bad and you have had to swim, your companions may be struggling to rescue you. Or you might have ignored all advice to the contrary, and gone paddling alone. If you can re-enter your boat while it is upside down, and roll up, you will have the ultimate self-rescue skill at your disposal.

You may be tempted to right the boat first, and then try to climb in. This is possible in an open canoe, but a narrow kayak is too unstable. You will also find that righting the boat allows water into the cockpit. If you re-enter and put the spraydeck on underwater, you may be able to roll up with less water aboard.

The technique for re-entry and roll is non-specific. You need to try it for yourself and work out the best way for you, but obviously, being able to roll already is a pre-requisite.

RE-ENTRY TIPS

• Put your paddles through the decklines of the kayak sideways. This helps to keep the boat upside down as you get in.
• Get right under the boat before trying to put your legs in. Start off by facing the stern, then back somersault into the cockpit. Think of it as a capsize drill in reverse.
• Remain calm and move slowly, so that none of your actions are wasted.

Re-entry Technique

1 Hold either side of the cockpit rim, push yourself down under the boat, and allow your legs to float up between your arms.

2 Push your feet into the cockpit, concentrating on staying directly under the boat. Try not to float up to one side.

3 Once your legs are in, get into the seat and put on your spraydeck (spray skirt). Grab your paddle and roll up.

Launching and Landing

Launching and landing skills are rarely required, but nonetheless are important because you are most likely to need them in an emergency situation. Practise them, and note the rules that apply in what can often be testing and difficult conditions.

While all paddlers should learn and practise how to seal launch into water from a height, touring paddlers will have less need of this skill, except in an emergency. Instead, sea paddlers need to be able to get afloat through waves on the sea, or a big lake or river that is large enough for the wind to produce some chop or swell.

In any type of boat it is important that you can launch and land effectively. In a touring boat, such as a sea kayak, that might be relatively fragile and

⌃ A double sea kayak setting out to sea from a public beach.

⌃ Even small waves require good technique and can upset the unwary.

heavily laden with supplies and rescue equipment, it is particularly important that you can do the job correctly. If a wave catches you sideways, you may lose control of your boat and capsize. Quite apart from it being a bad start to your fun day out, capsizing in very shallow water can cause you difficulties, and may even prove dangerous.

Launching Through Waves

Make sure that the boat is ready to launch, and that you have put in a drain plug (if required), secured the hatch covers, and tied down and protected your kit from the elements.

Next, put the boat down at the water's edge, pointing directly at it. If you are in a tidal area, remember that the tide might be coming in or going out, which could affect matters. If it is a heavy or tandem craft, make sure that you can move it towards the water without having to lift it, otherwise, once you get in, you might be stuck fast. And do not put the boat in

Launching Technique

1 Get into your kayak and attach the spraydeck when you are well above the waterline. Most paddlers find this easiest to do at the water's edge.

2 Move the kayak into the water, using your hands to lift yourself off the ground and push yourself along.

3 As soon as you are afloat, pick up the paddle and head out into the deeper water, propelling yourself forward with the paddle.

deep water where it can float because if you do it will be turned sideways by the waves, and can possibly knock you down or capsize. Once sideways to even small waves in shallow water, any boat becomes difficult to control. If you must manhandle it while afloat, stand on the seaward side.

Next, get into the boat quickly, and secure your spraydeck if you have one. Do not put your paddle down because it might be washed away. If you need both hands, secure the paddle under the deck-lines. If there are two of you, get into the boat one at a time.

Once in the boat, push it into the waves using your paddle on one side and hands on the other. Concentrate on keeping the boat at 90° to the waves, and then grab your paddle and get moving. Do not stop until you are so far out that the waves are not breaking. In particular, try to avoid capsizing in shallow water.

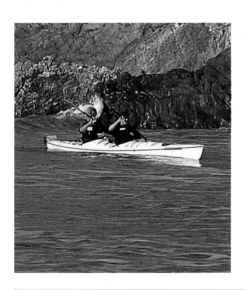

⌃ *Holding sea kayaks stready in preparation for landing.*

⌃ *This double kayak is preparing to land through waves.*

Landing Through Waves

The important point about landing a boat is to make sure you do not surf in on the front of a wave. Paddle in as close as you can while still allowing waves to pass underneath you. Even in small waves you might have to back-paddle to make sure they do not propel you shorewards, especially if the wind is onshore.

When you are as close to the shore as you can get, or are in danger of touching the bottom, paddle in on the back of a wave until your boat runs up the beach. Leap out as quickly as you can before the boat is sucked back with the returning wave, or before another wave comes in to turn your boat sideways. From here, you may be able to push yourself up the beach, using your hands, without getting out of the boat. Otherwise, jump out of the boat and pull it up through the shallow water on to the beach. Take care not to drop your paddle, or else it might be washed back into the sea.

Landing Technique

1 Wait for a wave to pass under your boat, then paddle in towards the shore on the back of the wave. Do not surf in on the front of the wave.

2 As the water gets too shallow for the boat to float, paddle on to the wave to get as far ashore as you can.

3 Push yourself safely ashore and jump out of the boat before any more waves come along. Keep hold of your boat, so that it doesn't get swept away by a wave.

ADVANCED PADDLING

SPECIALIST DISCIPLINES

Paddlers who achieve a high level of all-round skill and fitness tend to specialize in one or two disciplines: no one has the time to be an expert in more than a couple of fields. If you are looking for a speciality, the choice is wide — kayak or canoe, sea or inland, paddle or sail, freestyle or race. To help you make your decision, here are some key considerations. Two points to note are that, firstly, those disciplines with a competitive element are covered in more detail in the next section of this book. And secondly, with the possible exception of IC10 sailing, it will not be possible to attempt any of the following activities safely, with any hope of real success, until you are proficient at the skills covered so far.

*◖ Play paddling is the aquatic equivalent
of skate-boarding on land.*

*◗ Using a kite to power a double sea kayak.
This technology is still in its infancy.*

Extreme White Water Paddling

It is probably a lot more sensible to read about extreme kayaking than to try it, but if you really are tempted, the following gives a graphic description of what is involved. Danger is the key note, and the risks of serious injury are extremely high.

Extreme kayaking began around the 1970s, when paddlers first attempted white water descents so severe that if they fell out of the boat they were unlikely to survive. Usually listed as Grade (Class) 5+ or Grade 6 type waters, extreme paddling is characterized by large vertical drops or waterfalls.

The first practitioners were slalom paddlers because they already had the highly developed skills needed to tackle the difficult conditions. They were badly limited by their equipment, however. There was a limit to the volume of water or the size of drops they could tackle before their fibreglass boats disintegrated and pitched them into the water.

In retrospect, we know that the boats could have been made stronger then, but there was an obsession with light weight among performance-orientated paddlers. Perhaps this was justified because they invariably used 4m (13ft) long kayaks that became increasingly unwieldy as they got heavier.

As more boats were made from plastic, there was a significant shift in the world of extreme kayaking. First, the paddlers were able to attempt much more difficult conditions knowing that their boats were strong enough to withstand the water. Second, the foremost extreme white water paddlers were freestyle paddlers who had honed their skills doing the three-dimensional white water acrobatics that smaller, stronger boats made possible.

Assessing the Risks

The modern extreme kayaker is attempting water on which drowning or serious impact injuries are a constant threat. To stand any chance of survival he must use a boat that has been reinforced to prevent it from collapsing under the enormous pressure it must withstand, and have plate footrests with shock absorbers. Usually the boat will be very short.

Most kayakers now recognize that acceleration and manoeuvrability are far more important than outright speed. The boat will tend to be fairly rounded, and able to withstand impacts and potentially lethal pinning to which more pointed boats are susceptible. Extreme kayakers sometimes wear full face helmets such as those worn by motorcyclists, and even elbow pads and reinforced gloves. For instance, paddlers attempting long vertical drops might wear back supports to prevent spinal injuries.

Usually, tackling water this extreme is a team effort. While it is unusual for the paddlers to be able to help each other on the water, a rescue and support team in place on the banks will provide invaluable safety cover. All members of the team should be trained in first aid, and usually there will be at least one fully qualified doctor on hand. Climbing skills and equipment are often required to get paddlers to the top of a descent in order

 An open-boat canoeist running an extremely large waterfall.

to inspect the river beforehand. In some of the more extreme cases, when the geography makes climbing too difficult, helicopter support is used to inspect and gain access to the location.

Using all the skills and support at their disposal, modern extreme kayakers have successfully negotiated Grade 6 rapids that were thought impossible only a few years ago, and have paddled waterfalls more than 30m (100ft) in height without injury. However, there is always a fine line between success and failure, and a number of paddlers have died in far less extreme conditions. It is, therefore, hugely important to understand that such extreme and dangerous kayaking is only for a talented few who are supremely skilful, athletic, experienced, confident, determined and well-equipped.

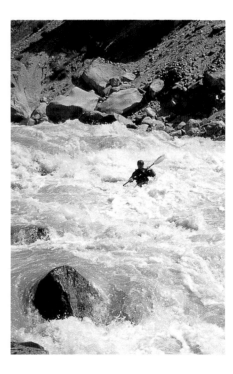

● *Steep and technical, this rapid holds all kinds of dangers. A moment's loss of control could lead to entrapment by the rocks or powerful hydraulics.*

● *This rapid looks so big and turbulent that even a big kayak is hurled end over end out of control as the kayaker battles with the might of the river.*

● *A Grade 5+ river with water seething over and around submerged rocks. To be upside down or swimming here would lead to certain injury.*

Play Paddling

As the name suggests, play paddling is the out-and-out playful side of paddling, where practitioners practise all kinds of fantastic tricks in what is the boating world's answer to roller-skating.

Play paddling began in slalom boats because skilful paddlers enjoyed trying to stand their boats on end in waves and stoppers. It was good practice for white water river running because it taught paddlers to cope with anything that the river could throw at them.

It was not until the plastic revolution of the early 1980s that play paddling gripped the imagination of the average recreational boater. Paddling these new and apparently indestructible boats, boaters were able to expose their craft to extraordinary feats and a level of pounding that had never before been possible. This was probably the most significant development in the history of paddle sport.

Today, play paddling and its competitive discipline, freestyle, means being so skilled at using a kayak or canoe in white water that all safety and survival considerations become second nature. In effect, the paddler is playing – frolicking in the waves and hydraulics, surfing, and performing acrobatic tricks using the power of the river.

Since the 1980s, nearly all white water paddlers have used play to exploit the power of the river. Their antics led to the development of kayaks and canoes that were specially designed for play paddling, and it subsequently transpired that experts could negotiate harder rapids in

these boats than they could in boats originally designed for more serious river running. This led to more people using play boats for all types of paddling and the development of new skills, spawning yet another generation of play boats.

This trend continued for the best part of 20 years. At the end of the twentieth century, play boats were relegated to what is known as park and play. This is a kind of extreme play paddling that revolves around taking your boat to a specific spot, playing there the whole time, and then going home without having run any rapids in the play boat.

◔ *A play paddler makes a wave-wheel down a rapid. Acrobatic tricks such as this are the main focus of play boating.*

The core play paddling activities are surfing river waves, and using hydraulics to perform vertical tricks, flipping the boat from end to end. These are the key skills, but the range of manoeuvres the expert can perform is bewildering. Virtually every river feature now facilitates some form of boat gymnastics. Many of the tricks are influenced by skate- and snow-boarding, and there is a culture of kayakers with their own music, dress code and jargon.

◔ *A twenty-first century play boat. This kayak is only 1.9m (6¼ft) long. It is designed to be dynamically unstable to facilitate aggressive acrobatic and aerial manoeuvres.*

Play Paddling Equipment

The essential equipment for play paddling is virtually the same as for any other white water routine. There are special park and play kayaks that resemble squirt boats, but they are made from plastic and have more volume in the centre to ensure that they are held by powerful hydraulics, while also having many of the safety features of a normal white water kayak. They are not terribly safe for general white water use but you can make good use of a general white water boat (especially a fairly recent one), for play paddling. A 1999 competition freestyle boat was still regarded as a good all-round white water kayak two years later, for instance.

It helps to have shorter paddles for play and freestyle paddling, but any strong white water paddle will do. A flexible shaft is a useful feature because this

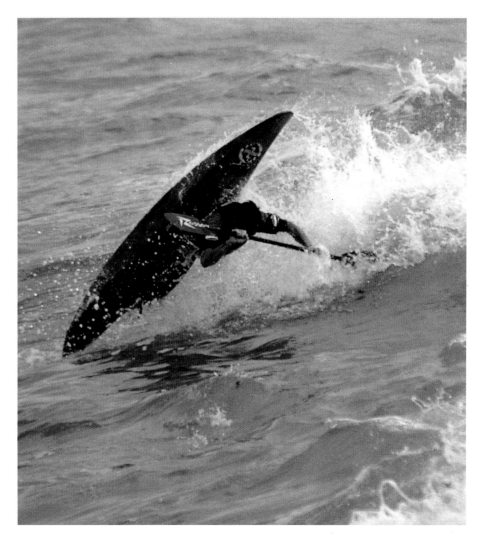

⊘ A big three-dimensional aerial manoeuvre, called a "kick flip", performed by the author, Bill Mattos.

⊘ The open canoeist, European Freestyle Champion, James Weir, paddling a massive stopper wave.

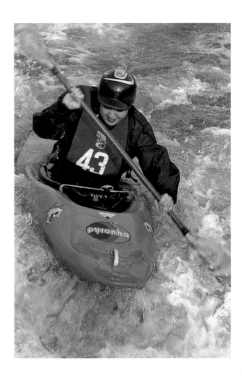

A play boater performs a cartwheel in a decked C1 freestyle canoe.

type of paddling is quite hard on the wrists. Most play boaters use a 45° feather on their paddles (feather is the term used to describe the angle between the two blades on a kayak paddle), a good compromise between the higher feather angles for long-distance paddling and the very low angles used by squirt boaters. Play paddling tends to wear down the paddle blades from paddling upstream in shallow water, and constantly scraping them across the boat.

What to Wear

Clothing is an important consideration for play paddlers because you will be regularly rolling and getting fully immersed in the water. Most play paddlers have the best spraydecks (spray skirts) and drytops money can buy. Safety, on the other hand, is less of an issue. Despite the undoubted danger of white

water, the play paddler tends to wear a fairly minimal buoyancy aid (personal flotation device, or PFD) because anything more would interfere with the flexibility needed for the play boater's gymnastic body movements. Helmets, unfortunately, often err on the side of fashion rather than total protection because play boaters try to avoid being thought of as too serious. It would be rare to find a play-boater with a throw-line or any other safety equipment in the boat, and many remove the end grabs from their boats, perhaps to improve the hydrodynamics, but more likely just to make the point.

This is the less responsible side of the sport. The appeal lies in the absence of many of the restrictions seen elsewhere, and the emphasis is on fun and dare-devil feats. It is worth adding, though, that play boating has a low accident rate, perhaps because of the extremely high skill level of the participants. It is not for novice paddlers.

Paddling into a stopper wave from downstream. The paddler's bib denotes permission to paddle on a commercial artificial white water course.

Play Paddling Etiquette

There is an accepted etiquette among play paddlers that differs from some of the rules normally observed on the river. White water paddlers usually focus on safety, which means giving way to anyone coming downstream, and letting other people join the front of an eddy wherever possible. However, these rules don't work very well for play paddlers. If a boater is playing on a wave or in a hole, they will not want to get out when another paddler approaches, but will expect the other paddler to be able to go around them. Similarly, play boaters tend to queue in the eddies to wait their turn on the wave, so to join the front of the eddy is jumping the queue, and not acceptable.

These variations work fine among like-minded individuals, because play paddlers are usually highly skilled, and they tend to stick to familiar sections of water that they can handle easily. The problems arise when paddlers of a different standard play on the same stretch of water, and when confident paddlers become impatient with others who are finding it a challenge just to survive. Whenever this situation occurs, both parties should be aware of the other's needs and accommodate them as much as possible. If this can't be achieved, one of the parties should agree to move to another stretch of water. Confrontations in the water are never acceptable because of the risk that someone will be hurt.

○ *A canoeist attempting a cartwheel stopper. Open canoes can perform amazing acrobatics in expert hands.*

○ *A play boater cruising around on a broken river wave before planning his next move.*

Squirt Boating

Squirt boating is a radical and very special type of paddling which appeared in the early 1980s, and had a profound influence on all kinds of white water boating. It added new levels of fun, especially when dipping the end of the boat under water.

A squirt boat is an extremely low-volume, lightweight kayak or canoe. In fact, squirt canoes are fairly rare, but should not be ignored. Most of the development of the squirt movement took place in kayaks, but the slalom canoeists contributed perhaps the most important idea of all, that of sinking the end of the boat in a controlled manoeuvre.

How It Developed

Slalom paddlers learnt to dip the ends of the boat, usually the stern, so that they could squeeze under the poles when negotiating difficult gates in a race or practice session. They quickly realized that this technique could also give them a dramatically quicker brake, turn and acceleration. It feels as though the water is storing up the energy carried into the

This squirt kayak shows just how flat and surfboard-like these low-volume boats are. The paddler's feet fit in the two bumps near the bow, and the knees in the two either side of the cockpit.

turn, which then feeds back into the boat as it accelerates away from the gate. And this is, indeed, how it works; the kinetic energy is stored as hydraulic energy, which converts back to kinetic energy. Paddlers quickly realized that swooping around the rapids, using these invisible dynamic forces, can be tremendous fun.

C1 (single-seater competition canoe) slalom boaters developed stern-dipping until they could easily get the bow above head height. Their K1 (single-seater

Bob Campbell, 1995 World Champion, surfing a wave on a cross-bow rudder. The unusual blade shape gives low resistance under the water.

competition kayak) counterparts were not far behind, despite having less leverage and the weight of their legs in front of them. At the time, the move was called a pivot turn. In the United States in the 1980s, kayakers experimenting with cut-down race boats likened the feeling to a wet bar of soap squirting out of the hand, and the name stuck. From then on, any move that involved sliding the end of the boat under the water was known as a squirt, and boats specifically designed to do it became squirt boats.

The American Influence

Largely because of the influence of two American brothers, Jim and Jeff Snyder, who were experts at the sport, the boats rapidly became smaller until they had to be custom-built to fit the paddler. The Snyder brothers were convinced that, as long as you had the requisite skills, a squirt boat could be used on any stretch of water provided it was not trapped on the surface by its own buoyancy. They called this the dense boat theory, and they proved their point by running some of the roughest white

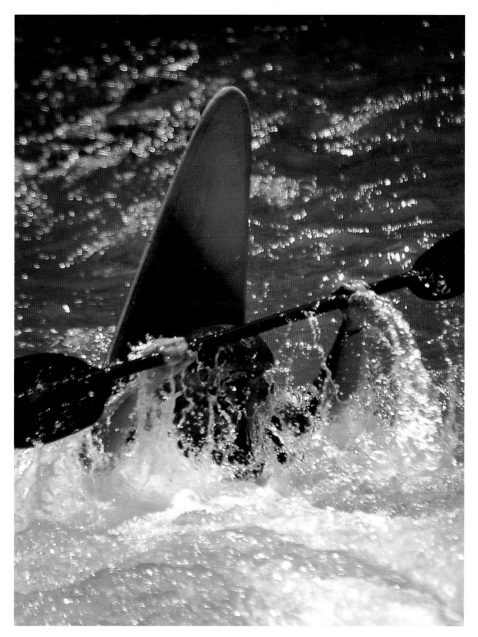

squirting techniques have been absorbed into the repertoire of the expert white water paddler.

These new techniques, and the evolution in boat design that they spawned, have been the driving force behind the transition from what is called old school white water paddling to the new school. They have made much of what was written or taught on the subject before about 1990 largely redundant. More importantly, though, it helped turn the sport of white water boating from one surrounded by issues of danger to one featuring fun, and for that we owe the founders a great debt.

Squirt Appeal

So why do squirt boaters choose to paddle these relatively dangerous boats. Why deliberately use a kayak that barely floats in green water, and take it into an aerated environment, where it will almost certainly spend most of its time underwater? This comes back to the aforementioned "dense boat theory".

A paddler who is comfortable with the white water environment finds that, so long as he can remain in control, a

⬑ *Top British squirt-boater Hazel Wilson doing a past-vertical cartwheel in the World Freestyle Championships, 2001.*

⬎ *A squirt-boater deliberately swipes at a rock in a flamboyant aerial move.*

water in the world in boats so small that they looked more like surfboards. They cartwheeled end over end on flat water, and performed the hallmark squirt boat trick, called the mystery move, where the paddler disappears completely below the surface to re-emerge at another place.

Shaping the Sport

Squirt boats are handmade in fibreglass or similar composite materials, and they have to be very strong to survive immersion in powerful water. Because of the way squirting has influenced white water boating, plastic play boats now bear a closer resemblance to squirt boats than they do to general-purpose boats from the pre-squirt era. Indeed, many play boats can now do cartwheels, and many

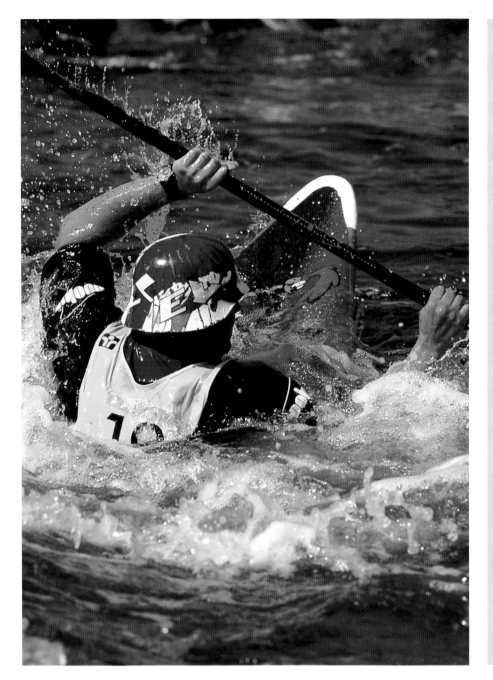

SQUIRT BOAT FACTS

• Squirt boats are about 2.5m (8¼ft) in length. The volume is designed to match the weight of the paddler, so that the boat is just above the point of neutral buoyancy.

• The boat is so flat that it needs special "tunnels" to accommodate the legs, and "bumps" for the feet.

• The paddler must be able to roll whenever necessary because getting out of the boat in an emergency is completely impractical. Most squirt paddlers use what is called a suicide block between their legs to stop undue body movement in the boat. This dramatically increases the wet exit time.

• Squirtists use very small paddles so that they can move them around easily underwater, constantly sweeping the blades across the deck. The paddles also have very low feather angles so that they can be turned to present no resistance to the current while underwater.

• The spraydeck (spray skirt) must make a perfect seal because the boat will become unmanageable, or even sink, if it ships any water at all.

• The paddler must always do a seal launch into the water because otherwise the boat is so low that it will fill up with water immediately, before the paddler has time to attach the spraydeck deck.

◓ *A squirt boater resurfaces from the water after momentarily disappearing in the so-called mystery move.*

◑ *Although squirt boaters invented the cartwheel, to perform one in a stopper like a conventional play boater, as here, is an extremely difficult feat.*

squirt boat is actually less likely to fall victim to hydraulics and other powerful water features. With minimal volume, the boat is almost "invisible" to aerated water, and responds only to the call of the green, allowing the pilot to navigate the solid currents of the river's heart without fear of turbulence and random transients.

to roll. Squirt boats are very sensitive to shifts in the paddler's weight, and this makes them prone to capsize. While squirt boats have performance advantages over other, high-volume designs, the consequences of any white water mishap are extremely serious. Entrapment, where part of your body or the boat gets stuck beneath the surface of the water, is the main danger for all white water paddlers because the strong currents can quickly pull you under. This is an even greater risk when paddling a squirt boat because

you are deliberately putting your boat in more precarious positions. These kayaks are physically difficult to get out of at the best of times, and to be seriously pinned in one would almost certainly prove fatal. In addition, the squirt boat is more prone to becoming pinned, and to planing to the bottom, by virtue of its wing-like shape. Drowned squirt boaters have been found still in their boats, with zigzag scratches on the hull a testament to their desperate attempts to lift an edge and unstick the craft from the bottom.

⊙ *Vertical gymnastics are another hallmark of the expert squirt boater. The boats themselves are low-volume and are highly sensitive to shifts in the paddler's weight.*

⊙ *The surfboard-like shape of the squirt boat lends itself to fast surfing and carving through the waves.*

Being made from stiff composite materials also makes the squirt boat a joy to paddle, compared to relatively soft and unresponsive plastic kayaks. The problem arises when things get out of control. To collide unexpectedly with a rock underwater is a nightmare for a squirt boater. Quite apart from the damage and injury it can cause, the loss of control can set off a chain of events that could end in disaster. So squirt boating is always practised in what are, for the expert paddler, extremely familiar and safe waters, so that the unexpected can never occur. Within the relatively safe confines of familiar rapids, the squirtists play unhindered by boat volume and the other limitations imposed on the more usual, surface-bound craft.

Squirting Safely

Paddlers should not attempt squirting until they are confident and quite expert at paddling an ordinary kayak. On top of this it is essential that they are able

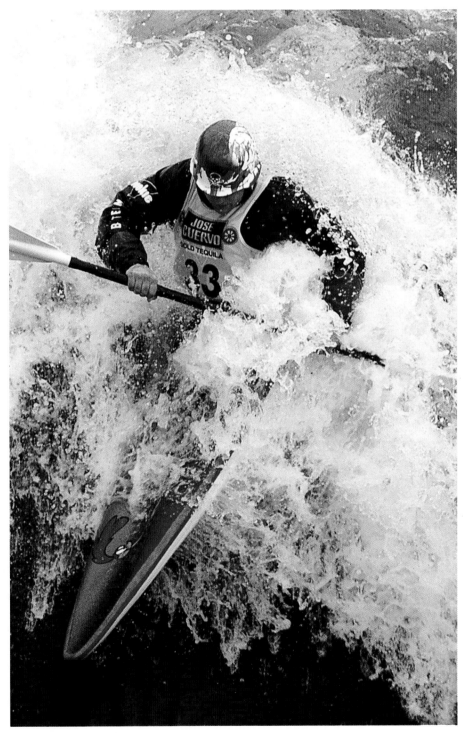

Kayak Surfing

In the latter part of the twentieth century, the explosion in the popularity of all kinds of surfing has meant that kayak surfers need to put some thought into how they go about taking a kayak out in the surf. Undeniably exhilarating, kayak surfing carries risks, and before you rush in, you need to practise in safe conditions. You must also learn the surfer's etiquette that respects the enjoyment and safety of other paddlers. Incidentally, surfing is one of the few disciplines that is not practised at any serious level in a canoe, despite the fact that the concept was almost certainly invented by canoe paddlers, thousands of years ago in Polynesia.

Riding the Waves

In most cases a wave will start to break at one point, and this breaking part will rush along the face of the wave until the whole wave is broken. The surfer takes off next to the breaking part, and rides along the wave on the green, unbroken face of the wave. He attempts to ride in the shoulder, or power pocket, where the breaking wave is at its steepest. Riding here provides the energy that gives the surfer enough speed to remain in control. If you are too far from the shoulder, you will not be able to ride fast enough and will be overwhelmed by the break. If you are too deep in the pocket, the same thing might happen. It is a balancing act that can only be learned from experience.

An inexperienced kayaker cannot go out in the surf safely unless he can roll repeatedly and well, and there is no one to collide with. After a little practice you can learn how to get off the wave when it has broken, and avoid being carried ashore by the soup, which is the broken white water that tumbles shorewards after the wave has collapsed. However, even a good paddler may have problems,

◔ *A kayak surfer hurtling along a steep, barrelling wave-face. This is skilful wave-riding at its best.*

and while you are bouncing in the soup you cannot ensure the safety of anyone paddling through the waves. If you hit them, it can mean serious injury. Do not attempt to come ashore where there are other people until you are experienced.

Spin Sequence

1 The kayaker is riding in the shoulder of the power pocket of a small wave. The breaking shoulder is on the left, the green part of the wave to the right.

2 The paddler uses the paddle and his edge control (which in this case comes mostly from the legs) to spin the boat around without losing any momentum.

3 The kayak continues to ride along the wave, still in the power pocket but now travelling backwards, ready to perform another trick.

⬆ An example of an aggressive top turn in a high-performance kayak. The wave is moving from right to left. The paddler is riding the power pocket towards the camera, and has turned (known as a cut-back) so as not to get too far from the shoulder of the wave.

Tricks of the Trade

A good surf kayaker can get fantastic rides, every bit as good as most board surfers, with the possibility of trying more tricks. Early surf kayaks were, unsurprisingly, based on slalom boats, and there is still an international competition class which has a minimum length limit of 3.5m (11½ft). These boats can be paddled fast, out through the waves, and can race incredibly quickly along the face of a wave, and perform long, carving turns rather like long surfboards.

More recently, many paddlers have taken to using white water play boats in the surf. Typically about 2.5m (8¼ft) long, these boats are not very fast between waves, but they do have the advantage of being able to jump over some very large broken waves, enabling the paddler to get more rides. The disadvantage of these boats is that they do not have enough speed to ride along the face of an ocean wave ahead of the breaking wave.

Wave Skis

Wave skis, a type of sit-on-top surf craft, had a spate of popularity in the 1980s. They were the first craft to provide spectacular leaping, aerial manoeuvres, but have now been replaced by the high-performance surf kayak – a 2.5m (8¼ft) boat which combines the best features of a wave ski boat, an international 3.5m (11½ft) boat, and a play boat. Surf kayaks often have surfboard-style fins to improve their grip and performance.

Essential Equipment

Kayak surfers use short paddles, usually about 1.85m (6ft) in length. They also need an extremely tough spraydeck (spray skirt) because the power of waves as they break is enormous, and will pull off all but the strongest decks. A helmet and flotation aid should be worn at all times, unless you are absolutely certain of your safety. They are recommended because swimming in the surf is unthinkable. An empty kayak is a dangerous projectile that could seriously injure you or other water users. Airbags can be used to fill up any space in the boat in case of a spraydeck implosion. Airbags prevent sinking and will make it easier for you to get the boat ashore: a boat that is full of water is heavy and difficult to move when totally submerged.

Taking Up Kayak Surfing

The best way to start is by watching the experts. When you try it, remember that you need good all-round kayak skills, and the ability to roll well. It helps considerably if you can first become proficient at white water paddling on rivers because, contrary to appearances, they are a good place to learn the basic boat skills from others who can coach from the eddy. In the surf, no one can really help you.

Once you are good at controlling the boat, lifting your leading edge, and surfing small river waves, you can practise these skills at sea, building up the size of the wave as you progress. Aim for a quiet spot, where there are few people around.

⌃ Twice World Kayak Surfing Champion Tim Thomas hurls a play boat into a spectacular exit manoeuvre.

⌃ Riding in the shoulder of a wave in a long International Class 3.5m (11½ft) surf kayak.

TIPS

• Do not go surfing in a kayak unless you can roll and have basic white water skills. Use a soft-foam wave ski craft to learn the principles.
• Notice how other surfers ride along the wave in the shoulder.
• Learn to get off the broken waves as soon as you can.

SURFING RULES

• Before you get into the water, sit on the beach and watch how other surfers ride it.

• Do not paddle out where other people are surfing. Wait until they have moved or paddle out elsewhere.

• Do not ride the soup unless there is no one between you and the shore.

• Do not take off on the same wave as someone else, unless you are on the other side of the break and you are sure you are going to ride away in opposite directions. Taking someone else's wave is called dropping in, and it is a surfing sin. The wave belongs to the first person to take off on it. If someone drops in on you, get off the wave, and afterwards explain the etiquette.

• If the surf is really crowded, go somewhere else, no matter how good a surfer you are.

◈ *A cut-back move in a play boat. These boats are widely used in the surf, despite being designed for river waves.*

◈ *A classic surfing shot. The author, Bill Mattos, riding in the power pocket under the breaking lip of the wave.*

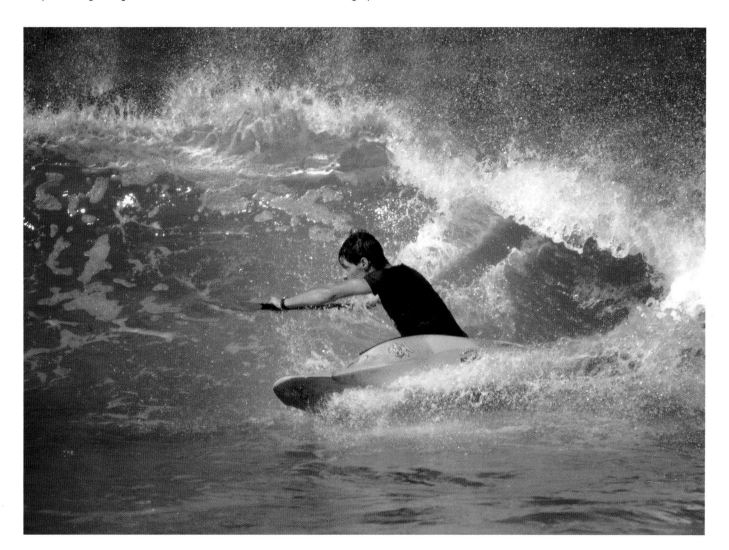

Canoe and Kayak Sailing

Using sails on canoes or kayaks is a new and challenging aspect of the sport. Still in its infancy, there are few dos and don'ts, but what you will need most of all are strong arms and plenty of confidence as you get whipped along at high speeds.

It is perfectly possible to use sails either to assist paddling or as the sole means of propelling a canoe or a kayak. It is not a formalized discipline because it is still in its experimental stage but it does, however, have a long history. Many books and drawings from the late nineteenth century feature canoes and other narrow craft with a sail being used to help propel it along.

Sails for canoes tend to have a swinging gaff-type rig. This can emulate a square rig, but tracking is a big problem. Kayaks are often fitted with a small Bermuda-style Delta-sail, which can help to support a paddled kayak, but it does

not offer any significant propulsion by itself. Some double sea kayaks are fitted with two of these sails. This is more effective because the sails are small enough that there is little likelihood of the craft being blown over by the wind,

A traditional sea kayak with the mast and sail stowed along the deck. When required, the mast can be stepped in a recess just in front of the cockpit.

and the double boats are so long that tracking is extremely good no matter what the weather is like.

Kites

A kite can be harnessed to a boat to support paddling. Kites are extremely powerful, and can pull a boat along at speed even in a light wind. Contrary to appearances, it is possible to sail at most wind angles provided the boat tracks quite well, but you need confidence in your ability as well as strength.

Now that two- and four-line kites have become commonplace, their use with canoes and kayaks has proliferated because the canopies have become more controllable. With a big 7.3sq m (24sq ft) kite or larger flexifoil design it is possible to make a double sea kayak plane along, but because the lateral force is considerable it would be very difficult to control a solo boat in this way. The advantage of a double is that one person can fly the kite, and the other can steer and brace with the rudder and paddle.

Experiments have been carried out with powerful kites and smaller, planing hulled kayaks. Still in its early days but demonstrating considerable potential, in kiting the emphasis is on excitement and aerial acrobatics.

Launching a Kite

1 When the wind is up, inflate the buoyant chambers of the kite.

2 DO NOT tie the kite lines to the boat or to yourself: this is potentially lethal.

3 Pay out the lines. This kite is designed to be launched from the water surface.

4 As the wind fills the canopy, hang on tightly. It could be a wild ride!

⊙ *Two sea kayaks with small sails. There is a batten near the top, so that a square sail becomes more like a gaff rig with a mini topsail.*

⊙ *Sailing downwind. The paddle is being used as a rudder here, but could equally act as a keel when reaching, i.e. sailing across the wind.*

TIPS
• Small sails can be used to assist while paddling a kayak manually.
• Larger sails will require that you concentrate on steering the boat using the paddle.
• Make sure that if the kayak capsizes, you will be able to unstep the mast and roll up.
• The sail can be rolled around the mast, and both mast and sail can be stowed on the deck when the kayak is being paddled.

Sailing IC10

This obscure and eccentric feature of the competitive canoeing scene is included here more for its historical than its contemporary relevance. Many people wonder why it counts as canoeing at all because the boat requires a sailing dinghy and paddles are not necessary. But canoeing it is, and if it is excitement that you are looking for, sailing IC10 really does have it all.

 Two IC10 boats racing on Lake Windermere in England. The boat bears little resemblance to a canoe.

What Is IC10?

The International Canoe 10 Square Metre was, until recently, the fastest single-handed sailing craft in the world. Nowadays, a variety of sail-boards and a handful of high-tech modern dinghies go faster, but it is still an amazing craft both to sail and to watch, requiring an incredible degree of skilful handling, balance, athleticism and agility. There is probably nothing else like it in the sports of sailing and paddling when it comes to the wide range of talents required for good control and handling.

The IC10, as it is sometimes known, is a sophisticated boat in a traditional form. Its name comes in part from its 10sq m (100sq ft) sail area, but how it resembles a canoe, except in the narrowness of its hull and consequent instability, is more of a mystery. The IC10 has a 5.2m (17ft) long hull weighing 63kg (139lb). The helmsman has a sliding seat on rails that can be extended up either side of the boat, allowing him to shift his body weight in and out. It replaces the wire trapeze system found on more modern dinghy designs. This, in combination with the narrow hull and relatively large sail area, allows the boat to reach speeds in excess of 30km per hour (19mph) in a stiff following breeze.

How It Developed

The sliding seat concept has its origins in the Native American open canoe. While there is no evidence that sailing these boats was ever commonplace, the paddling technique involved sitting outside the up-wind gunwale on a plank of wood, to stop the high-sided boats being blown over by the wind. The strength of the wind would be described as "it's a two-plank day" or a "three-plank day", depending on how many people had to sit out on the plank to keep the boat stable. This appears to be the tradition that led eventually to the development of the sailing canoe as we know it.

Perhaps not surprisingly, given its American origins, the sport of IC10 is especially popular today in the United States. In competitions in the United States, there used to be a so-called "paddling leg", in which the canoe would be sailed around the course for one lap and paddled for the next. The paddling aspect is new rarely included.

The shape of the IC10 hull is strictly determined by competition regulations, but competitors are at liberty to adjust the sail and rig design to optimize the boat's performance, as long as the total sail area does not exceed the stipulated 10sq m (100sq ft). In the latest high-performance sailing dinghies, the sail is usually fully battened from top to bottom.

⬆ *A wooden sailing canoe. The sliding seat system can be clearly seen.*

⬇ *Two IC10s on a reach. Note the narrow hull design, and the sailors with their weight right outside the boat.*

As a championship discipline, overseen by the International Canoe Federation (ICF), IC10 boats are sailed by men or women of 69–95kg (152–210lb) in weight, and of 19–60 years of age. To win, sailors must have all the skill and determination of motor-racing drivers, knowing how to use the wind and tides, while being tactically aware, and knowing how to prepare and tune the rig to give the best possible performance.

The racing of IC10 boats is governed by the ICF and national canoeing bodies. World Championships are held tri-annually, and national championships annually in many countries worldwide.

COMPETITION EVENTS

After World War I European skiing enthusiasts, who were starting to paddle white water for sport, came up with a new idea — the format for slalom and down-river racing that we see today. And much later, towards the end of the twentieth century, developments in boat design became the prime movers behind a whole range of more recent competitive events such as polo, kayak surfing and freestyle.

In turn, these events have led to an increasing emphasis on training, coaching and, in particular, psychology in order to improve performances. It would now be very difficult for even a talented individual to compete without attention to these issues. While theory is certainly important, there is no substitute for time spent paddling your boat as a way of increasing your experience.

What follows is general information on the nature of, and requirements for, today's major competitions. The best way to get involved in a competition is to approach your local kayak or canoe supplier, who will recommend a club that practises your chosen discipline. For all of the events mentioned in the following pages, you will need to be skilled with the paddle and, in some cases, will have to acquire better techniques and more experience before you can begin to compete, but do not let this put you off.

◑ *A paddler performs his manoeuvre on a rapid while other competitors wait their turn.*

◐ *Competitive paddling makes excellent spectator viewing for the whole family.*

Slalom

For plenty of spills and thrills, you cannot beat slalom. Racing downstream, through a series of gates, it tests racers on three levels, demanding great technical skill, strength to manage the boat, and superb concentration because highly accurate decisions about which stroke to make have to be made at fantastic speed.

Inspired by the sport of slalom skiing, which is a race downhill in which the skier must negotiate a large number of gates, European skiers came up with the idea for kayak and canoe slaloms. They needed something to replace their own sport in summer when the snow melted.

Racing the Clock

The sport is a time trial. One paddler at a time attempts to negotiate a predominantly downstream course on a white water river, marked out using gates through which they must pass. Each gate consists of two vertical poles suspended from wires. All the gates are numbered; green and white gates must be paddled in the downstream direction, while red and white gates must be paddled upstream.

The object is to paddle the course as quickly as possible without touching the gates or missing any. If you do either, penalty seconds are added to your time by the gate judge. Each competitor will

⬇ *A British duo racing a double-seater competition canoe, or C2, in France.*

have one or more practice runs, and then two timed runs. The best of the two times counts towards the final result.

Competition Categories

There are a number of categories, including men's and women's kayak (K1) classes, and single and double-decked canoe (C1 and C2) classes. There is no separate women's class for canoe events. The kayaks must be 4m (13ft) in length and at least 60cm (2ft) in width; in the C1 class they must be the same length and at least 70cm (28in) wide. The C2s are 4.58m x 80cm (15ft x 31½in). Juniors classes use the same size boats as the adults. There is also often a team event in which a team of three paddlers negotiates the course at the same time. The team is timed from the first to start to the last to finish. All three paddlers must finish within 15 seconds of each other, and all their penalties are added to the time.

◔ *Manoeuvring skills and stamina are the key to the slalom paddler's success.*

◔ *A K1 slalom paddler. The bent paddle shaft is popular among slalom kayakers.*

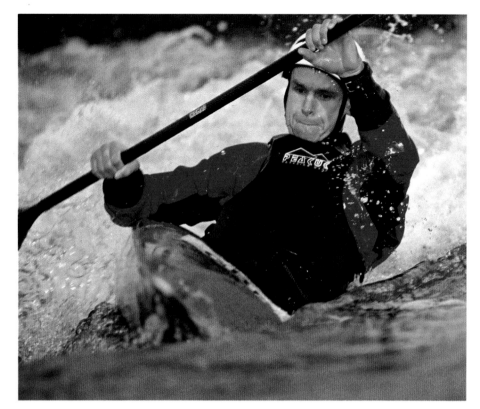

Taking Up Slalom

If you want to become involved in slalom, you will need to join a club that has some members who are interested in this field. Not all canoe clubs have slalom paddlers as members, let alone a slalom coach. It would be very difficult to get to grips with it on your own, so seeking out the society of fellow slalomists is pretty essential if you wish to progress.

There are no skill pre-requisites, since the techniques for paddling a slalom boat are the same as for flat water paddling, and can be learnt in a competition craft, even if you have never paddled any kind of canoe or kayak before.

There are also divisional systems in most countries, which means you do not have to compete against national champions unless you are at that level!

Slalom Kayaking

Slalom kayaks are extremely lightweight boats made from carbon and/or Kevlar™. Hence, they are fragile considering the environment they are used in, but slalom paddlers are adept at dodging obstacles.

Slalom used to be the natural choice for anyone skilful at white water paddling and who had the urge to compete but, sadly, participation has declined since the introduction of plastic kayaks. The plastic boats have allowed more people, and in particular less skilful ones, to go paddling white water without fear of the consequences. However, slalom has been included in the Olympic Games intermittently since 1972, and it remains one of the few paddling disciplines to be well known to the general public. It is an extreme test of strength, skill and concentration, and is unlikely to be dislodged from its position as the world's premier canoeing and kayaking discipline, because of it's profile, status, and the fact that the whole family can enjoy watching the competition events in a controlled and safe environment.

⊙ *Using a stopper wave to help make the fastest line between gates.*

⊙ *This kayaker has exited a wave so fast that his lightweight boat is almost launched clear of the water.*

⊙ *A C2 slalom crew competing at World Championship level.*

Specialist equipment is not required - the same basic equipment that you would use when you first start paddling is fine for slalom initially, although you will find that most slalom paddlers aspire to close-fitting garments and gear that emphasizes light weight, and acquire such items as soon as possible. The boats themselves are relatively expensive compared to plastic recreational canoes and kayaks, but you do not need to have a top-flight slalom boat right away. In fact, you will usually be able to borrow boats for the first few seasons from a club that offers coaching in slalom. Contact your local paddling stockist for information.

◔ *This paddler has just cleared a gate but is careful not to touch the pole with his elbow or paddle blade.*

◑ *Note the intense concentration on the face of this Italian slalom competitor.*

SLALOM FACTS
• Slalom is the original white water sport, and is still one of the few Olympic paddlesport disciplines.
• The following are the only classes available to the slalom racer:
  MK1 – men's single kayak
  LK1 – ladies' single kayak
  C1 – single canoe (unisex)
  C2 – double canoe (unisex
      or mixed).
• Top slalom paddlers train in the boat every day as well as gym- and cross-training.
• In an entire event, a racer might have only three two-minute runs down the course.
• Slalom boats are 4m (18ft) long, which makes them almost twice as long as a white water playboat. In addition, the slalom boat weighs only half as much as a modern plastic white water boat.
• A slalom course is designed to test all of the basic white water skills, such as breaking in and out, ferry glide, S-cross, and using currents and water features to full advantage. It is also a test of the fitness and power of the athlete.

River Racing

River racing, which includes wild water and rapid racing, is another competitive class that was first promoted primarily by European skiers. If slalom equates to slalom skiing, then river racing is the equivalent of downhill racing on skis.

Like slalom, the sport has strict regulations governing the design and dimensions of the boat, and the way the races are held.

Rules and Boat Shapes

Wild water racing (WWR) regulations are laid down by the International Canoe Federation, paddle sport's regulating body. These require the boats to have a maximum length of 4.5m (15ft) and minimum width of 60cm (2ft) for the K1 class, 4.3m x 70cm (14ft x 28in) for C1, and 5m x 80cm (16ft x 31½in) for C2. These maximum lengths are necessary because, generally speaking, the longer a boat is, the faster it is; similarly, the narrower the boat, the faster it is. These lengths in turn have led to homogeneous designs where all the craft are identical in dimensions and are extremely similar in overall shape.

River racing boats have a deep, vertical bow for slicing through waves, a narrow hull for speed, and a wide deck, which creates the minimum width while also

⊙ A white water racing C1 and K1. The boats are extremely similar but for the kneeling/sitting issues and the paddles used. The easiest way to tell the boats apart is by the fact that the canoe has a smaller, rounded cockpit.

◁ These racers are preparing for a practice run. Note the high bow and flared hips of their boats.

providing the necessary volume to stop the boat rearing up when punching through hydraulic water. The wide back deck tapers rapidly again to a pointed, vertical tail to give a clean, turbulence-free passage through the water. That is why the racing boat looks very strange, and quite different from any other canoe or kayak around today.

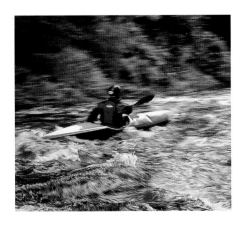

🔼 *The downstream speed of the river racer is apparent in this photograph.*

They are usually made from high-tech composite materials such as carbon and/or Kevlar™, and are therefore extremely light and fragile. Some manufacturers produce plastic replica river racing boats that are suitable for learning and training in.

Handling the Boat

Wild water boats are quite unstable compared to slalom or play boats, but are not as wobbly as flat water racing boats.

🔽 *Breaking in and out of the current at speed is not easy in a river racer.*

They turn fairly responsively when leant to the outside of the turn, and can make dramatic changes in direction, using what is called a wave top turn, but with the full length of the hull in the water they are more directional than manoeuvrable.

Reading the water is an important skill for any white water paddler, but in racing it is absolutely essential to spot the fastest line down a rapid.

All steering must be done with leans, or with strokes that drive the boat forward rather than slowing it down. There is a rhythm to the forward paddling which attempts to make all the strokes when the boat is going up a wave, and not down. This helps a lot with speed and endurance, and stops the nose of the boat from getting buried in white water, and slowed down, any more than is absolutely necessary.

The most important part of river racing is to avoid both rocks and eddies. Hitting a rock in a lightweight Kevlar™ racing boat would almost certainly result in damage, and may well sink the boat. Clipping an eddy can cause the boat to spin round and out, which results in lost time. With practice and observation, you will find the best and fastest way down, and make no mistake, it is a wild ride.

River Races

Wild water races are run as time trials over a section of Grade (Class) 3, or higher, rapids. Rapids up to Grade 5 have been used for top-class events. The rapids rarely demand special skills, however, because of the length of the boats and their lack of manoeuvrability. The course takes 20 minutes to complete, and competitors start at one-minute intervals. This means that sometimes racers will overtake each other, which makes for extra excitement.

Rapid racing is identical to wild water racing, except that the course is more of a sprint, only one or two minutes long. It was designed for spectator appeal, and at some venues two boats at a time race each other. Rapid racing represents an attempt by the organizers of river racing events to attract interest, from the media and potential participants, to a sport which, like slalom, has declined dramatically since the growth of informal play paddling.

Taking up River Racing

The best way to get involved in river racing is to join a club that has a strong tradition of the sport. Get into a WWR boat and paddle it regularly to get used to the way these strange beasts behave.

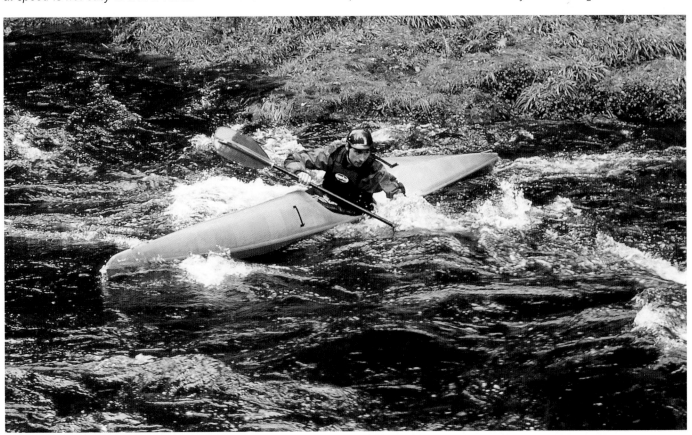

Freestyle

Freestyle is the name given to competition play paddling. Originally called rodeo, it was conceived in the 1980s and has grown to be one of the biggest competitive canoeing and kayaking disciplines in many countries.

The original concept came from the common boating practice of taking turns to show off your best trick or ride in a hole, or on a wave. It was not long before informal competitions sprang up, with paddlers voting for the best performance. The skill level soon increased dramatically and more formal competitions were organized, with independent judges. For a long time it was not taken too seriously because the paddlers did not take themselves too seriously.

But, at the end of the twentieth century, freestyle became almost as rigidly formalized as other competition events, like slalom. There is now an accepted

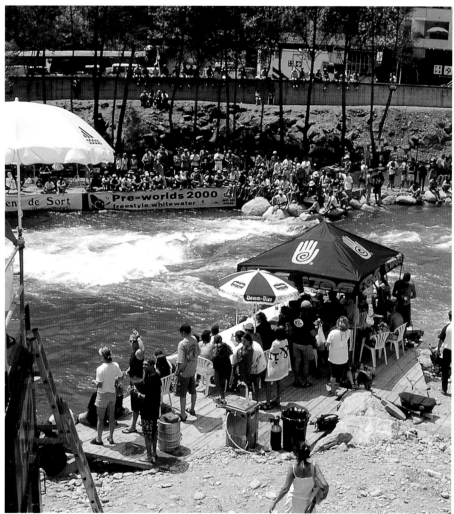

● *A British Junior competing in the 2000 Pre-World Championships.*

◄ *An overview of an international competition scene. The competition stopper (hole) is clearly visible.*

structure – paddlers have a set period of time on a wave or in a water feature, and will attempt to perform as many complex tricks as possible in that time. The exact method for scoring these moves changes every year as the sport evolves, but the basic principle is as follows.

Technical Scoring

For every 180° transition (change of direction) from upstream to downstream, or vice versa, the paddler will be awarded technical points. If it is a flat transition (or spin) the score will be 1 point. An elevated transition (higher than 45°) will score 2 points, and a vertical transition will score 4 points.

It is worth noting that transitions from being sideways on in the wave to being sideways on facing the other way, or side-surf to side-surf, do not count because most failed moves will end up looking like that in any case.

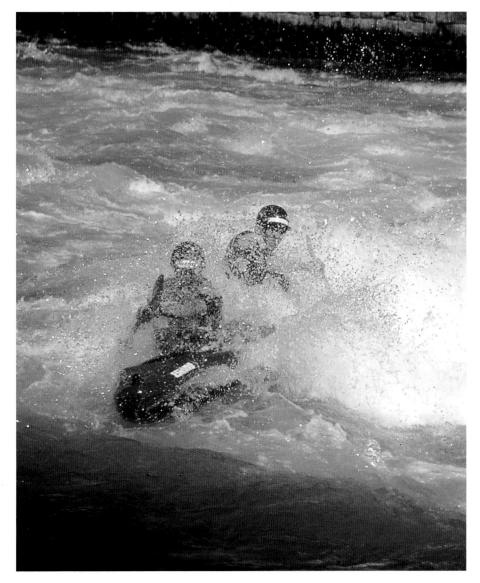

The Classes

Freestyle has separate classes for Men, Ladies and Juniors, as do most other competitive disciplines, and it also has other classes for different boat types. Here are the main classes that you will usually find included in a freestyle event.

K1 (Solo Kayak) – Float Freestyle boats that are not squirt boats are usually called float boats because they float on the water, while squirt boats do not. Over the years, float boats have become more and more like squirt boats in their design, until the only discernible difference is that the float boats float.

A definition of a float boat is that you can get in one on flat water with no spraydeck (spray skirt), without the boat shipping any water. The cockpit area is usually the only part of the boat that has enough volume to remain consistently above the water. K1 float is usually the biggest class in any freestyle event.

Decked C1 These boats are usually identical to the competition kayaks, or K1s, except that they are propelled by a canoe paddle used in the kneeling position. The performance of these freestyle canoes is now so astonishing that they are outscoring kayaks. This is partly because the advantages of the paddling position outweigh the disadvantages for an expert, and partly

◉ *A K2 crew competing in a freestyle event in Thun, Switzerland. These paddlers have missed the wave and are paddling for the eddy in an attempt to re-establish before their time runs out.*

◉ *A competitor initiating a cartwheel in a stopper during a freestyle competition.*

There will also be a variety score. The judges have a list of tricks that are established moves and have names, such as the spin, cartwheel, splitwheel and blunt. Each additional trick performed in the ride adds to the technical score. The result is that the paddler tries to do as many transitions as possible in the ride, while incorporating as many different moves as possible. This ensures that you cannot win by simply cartwheeling (flipping the boat end over end) non-stop for the entire run.

An open canoe paddler in a freestyle event. He is surfing the wave, and uses his hand to initiate a turn rather than try a cross-bow stroke with the paddle!

because practitioners can score so many clean moves (tricks performed without a paddle stroke), by virtue of the fact that they only have one paddle blade to use.

Open C1 The freestyle open boat is a controversial class. The rules ensure that the boat must be fairly close in design to a traditional open boat, and this makes it quite hard to do any modern freestyle moves. Many people feel that the open boat is being left behind as the other freestyle classes develop, but it still remains the most crowd-pleasing freestyle discipline because is it so simple and spectacular.

Squirt C1 and K1 The definition of a squirt boat is that it will ship water if you sit in it on flat water without a spraydeck. Squirt boating is responsible for the invention of most of the moves we see in freestyle today, although sadly it is really quite rare to see one being paddled canoe style. Unfortunately the lack of volume, or buoyancy, in a squirt boat makes it less retentive in a hydraulic, which means it barely floats. However, these minimal-volume craft make up for that with their smoothness and style, and their signature manoeuvre, the mystery move, where the paddler disappears from view below the water surface and re-emerges at another place.

Freestyle – in Design and Competition

No other canoeing and kayaking discipline today has the profound and widespread influence that freestyle has. The vast majority of white water boats sold today are identical to, or are based upon, the latest freestyle designs, even though they are unsuitable for their owner's activities. It is just like the heyday of slalom, when nearly all the boats used on white water were essentially based on slalom designs.

Unfortunately, it looks as if freestyle may suffer the same fate as slalom and become marginalized by its own rigid adherence to a competitive structure, deviating further and further from the latest thinking in general recreational paddling. As soon as it becomes a competitive discipline only, rather than a fun pastime, it will, like slalom, become a sport for a limited number of special enthusiasts. Many of the proponents of freestyle recognize this danger, and have begun to turn a new branch of the play paddling skills repertoire into the sport of extreme racing.

Scoring Freestyle Moves

Exactly how the judges award points for paddling moves will depend on the rules of the particular competition. However, there is a generally accepted score sheet. The following moves are given in ascending order, arranged by difficulty and hence technical score.

Surf

Planing in control on a standing wave or in a hole with the bow pointing upstream.

Backsurf

The same as surf, but with the stern facing upstream.

Spin

From frontsurf to backsurf, or vice versa. A 360° spin scores as 2 x 180°s.

Clean Spin

A 360° spin made with just one stroke will score higher than a spin.

Vert or "End"

A 180° direction change with one end of the boat elevated out of the water throughout. There are three scoring levels: up to 45, up to 75, and 75–105 (which would be called "past vertical"). A vert can be performed either on the bow or on the stern.

◔ Paddlers in the eddy wait their turn. The paddler in the hole is either warming up or has commenced his run.

◔ These two paddlers are not actually competing, but are having fun during a break by crossing over one another as they surf in the hole.

Cartwheel

This is a continuous transition from front end (bow) to back end (stern).

Clean Cartwheel

This is performed with the second end achieved without the paddle in the water. The boat is moved using the legs.

Superclean

A full cartwheel performed without making any use of the paddle at all for the duration of the move.

Splitwheel

A cartwheel with an edge change between the two transitions.

Pirouette

A 360° spin around the axis of the boat while it is standing on (either) end.

Loop

Somersaulting the boat end over end with the deck presented flat to the current (a cartwheel would be on edge).

Blunt

An elevated transition on a green wave.

Air Blunt

The same as a blunt but with the entire boat clear of the water.

Kickflip (or California Roll)

An aerial barrel roll.

Extreme Racing

Extreme racing is, at the time of writing, the newest form of specialist competitive discipline to gain widespread publicity. Though it sounds incredibly dangerous, it is not that alarming, though you will need high skill levels to try it.

Usually run over a section of Grade (Class) 4 rapids, extreme racing is a modern incarnation of what white water racing used to be – a race down rapids which, though extreme for an inexperienced paddler, is well within the capabilities of an expert. Perhaps because of its perceived danger level, it is now mainly practised by professional boaters. It is not, however, as extreme as the descents attempted by those who push the limits of extreme kayaking.

⊙ *This paddler's face shows the effort as he sprints a fairly flat section during an extreme race.*

◐ *The power of the hydraulic at the base of this fall makes the bow of the boat rear up, and the paddler has to fight for control of the boat.*

History of Extreme Racing

Extreme racing as we know it today grew out of the shortcomings of freestyle as a media flagship for canoeing and kayaking. In fact, people had been racing down rapids for many decades, whether in specialist racing boats or in informal competitions using general-purpose craft. This probably attracted more media attention than most paddle sport events, but in the mid-1990s top freestyle paddlers, already established as the most skilful and extreme boaters in the world, began to look at the fun race events that often ran alongside freestyle get-togethers with renewed interest.

These events were more popular with the crowds and the media than any freestyler gyrating inexplicably in a hydraulic, so people began to organize races down what was, for them, quite manageable white water, but which could be billed as extreme. This 1990s buzzword attracted big crowds and advertising. At first, these races were by invitation only, and just a few paddlers competed but, as the idea began to catch on, more people participated.

How to Take Part

To consider participating in extreme racing, you need to be totally confident at paddling Grade 4 and 5 rapids, and tackling waterfalls (albeit fairly safe ones) up to 10m (33ft) in height. There are currently no rules about the type of kayak you should use. Unlike white water racing, the emphasis is on what is possible and not the best time achieved by a boat

This paddler has taken an unusual and very risky line to try to stay on the top flow of this folded drop.

Sprinting through turbulent rapids in a European extreme race.

within set rules. Most paddlers use river-running or crossover play boats that are equipped for extreme paddling with full plate footrests, airbags, and plenty of padding.

The best extreme racers in the world currently seem to be top freestyle paddlers, but this may well change as more people begin to train specifically for racing. This is the likely trend because extreme racing seems the most likely kind of paddle sport to attract major sponsorship and prize money. In the meantime, however, you cannot simply go along to your local canoe club and tell them that you want to get involved in extreme racing. Instead, go white water paddling and freestyling, and get plenty of valuable experience. If you see an event advertised in the paddling press, you will have an opportunity to test out your skills.

Sprint and Marathon

Paddlers are always looking for new thrills and ways of racing, and sprint and marathon provided plenty of action. The two disciplines are accessible and attractive to all ages and abilities.

Paddling fast boats on flat water, or sometimes moving water has been a part of the canoe and kayak scene from the very outset. Pick any sports activity, and there will always be lots of people who want to adapt it for racing, and paddle sport is no exception.

Sprint racing is incredibly popular, and is a time trial over a fixed distance from a standing start. There are categories for K1 (solo kayak), K2 (double kayak) and the spectacular K4 (four-seater kayak), and races are over 500m, 1000m or 10,000m. The maximum for a Ladies race is 5,000m. There are similar categories for canoes with C1, C2 and C4, all paddled with a single blade in a high drop-knee position, which is half kneeling, on one foot and one knee.

Marathon is very similar to sprint, but the distance could be anything from 10km (6 miles) to the mammoth 200km (125 miles) Devizes to Westminster race, which is held every year in the United Kingdom, or the Arctic Canoe Race that is over 1,000km (620 miles) long.

◐ *An older and more stable K1 still shows a fair turn of speed.*

◐ *A paddler holds on to the jetty as he adjusts the spraydeck (spray skirt) in his unstable racing kayak.*

The fundamental difference between sprint and marathon is that sprint boats usually race on a lake and in a straight line, whereas the marathon is a journey, and might involve negotiating bends and getting out of the boat to carry it around weirs, rapids or other impassable sections of river. In some races, such as the British Exe Descent and the Irish Liffey, competitors might even tackle large drops and rapids in their wobbly racing boats in order to avoid walking around them.

Race Criteria and Skills

Single racing boats are about 5.2m (17ft) long and 50cm (20in) wide, although the double boats are longer to accommodate two paddlers, at about 6.5m (21ft).

You have to get in fairly carefully, putting your feet squarely in the middle of the boat and keeping some weight on your hands, but once you get moving it will be more stable. Marathon kayaks are fitted with a rudder, which is operated by the feet, because, while the boats are good at running in straight lines, nothing you do with the paddle seems to make much difference to the course. This is unlike most kayaks in which you expend a great deal of energy trying to make them run straight ahead.

While the rudder is effective at steering the boat, it does interfere with the rhythm of paddling, and is actually much more useful for offsetting a constant veer caused by a cross-wind, for example, than for making any changes in direction. Luckily the boats are responsive to slight leans: lean a little to the left, and it veers quite dramatically to the right, and vice versa. This allows you to do a lower, more sweeping stroke on the outside of the turn and a good high stroke on the inside. Because the boat is so narrow that it encourages a vertical paddling action, with lots of body rotation without too much effort from the arms, it is highly efficient for long-distance paddling.

The racing boat is quite unresponsive to most kayaking strokes apart from a really good forward paddling action. A low brace will be required to keep the boat balanced; placing the back of the blade flat on the water provides some support. Otherwise, you will not need to do much except paddle and lean, and anticipate when to turn, because large circles are the rule for these courses.

◗ *This K2 marathon crew uses the rudder to approach the bank for a portage. The stern paddler is trailing a low brace to keep them stable.*

Equipment and Safety

You need very little additional equipment except for the paddle, which should probably be a modern asymmetric design to facilitate a fast, long paddling action.

The usual test for paddle length is to stand the paddle up in the shop – you should just be able to reach and grip the top of the blade without having to stretch. It is worth spending a lot on a paddle to make sure that you get a good one that is light with slightly less than a 90° feather (the angle between the two blades of a kayak paddle). A full 90° will eventually place quite a strain on the wrists, but because much less causes a lot of wind resistance, settle for 70–80° if you can. The rule with paddles is try before you buy. Serious racers use wing paddles, a specialist type that provides high efficiency and lift, but these are initially very difficult to use and you will need a lot of practice before you can use one effectively.

A spraydeck (spray skirt) is sometimes used as small waves splash into the cockpit even on flat water, or you could simply opt for a decent sponge. And,

generally speaking, racers do not wear buoyancy aids (personal flotation devices) unless they are juniors, but this is because rescue is always at hand at the course. You should wear a flotation aid when training for a race because it can be fairly difficult to recover a swamped racing boat alone, and your friends will not be able to offer much apart from moral support. Furthermore, hardly anyone ever drowns while wearing a buoyancy aid. Unless you have taken other steps to ensure your safety, you should use one.

You should also wear shoes that you are not too heavy amd are safe to swim in, and take a drink of water or energy drink in the boat. You can end up quite dehydrated paddling a kayak, and when you are racing a boat it is very easy to forget how long you have been in the water. Being thirsty over a short period of time will not kill you, but it will negate many of the benefits of doing exercise.

The best way to get involved is to attend a club that specializes in sprint or marathon racing and training. Ask your local kayak supplier to recommend one.

Canoe Polo

Canoe polo is an aquatic ball game similar to water polo. Despite its name, it is not played in canoes but in kayaks that are known as polo boats. It is a fast, lively team game, nearly as good to watch as to play.

You need two teams of five players who endeavour to pass or carry a football-sized ball and throw it in the opposing goal, a square net that is 1.5m (5ft) wide by 1m (3½ft) high, suspended 2m (6½ft) above the water. The goals are placed at each end of a stretch of water, which is marked out to form a pitch, the dimensions of which can vary. The pitch can be delineated on any stretch of water, but will often be in a swimming pool. Canoe polo originated separately in a number of different places and in different ways.

Chasing and playing with a ball is an excellent way of learning good boat control skills while focusing on the ball rather than on the boat. This sub-conscious learning is a terrific way of developing and reinforcing the skills required to pilot a kayak successfully,

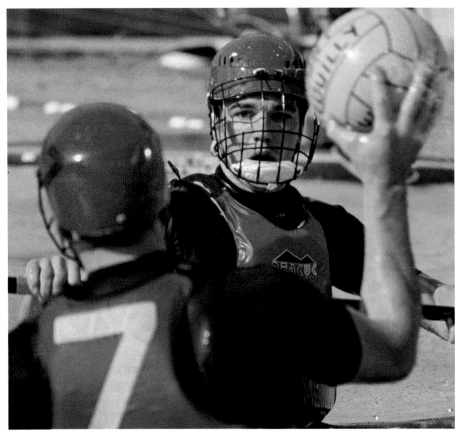

◔ A polo player scoops up the ball to pass. Note the flotation aid and helmet.

◔ Two players face off. The wire face guard is absolutely essential.

and because it was commonly used as a learning tool by instructors, it developed into a game, particularly in Britain, France and Australia. In 1989, the International Canoe Federation (ICF) accepted polo as one of its recognized paddle sports, and merged and adapted the different rules from various countries to create a set of international rules common to all ICF member nations.

Rules and Regulations

The game now has a strict set of regulations. Crash helmets are compulsory, as are buoyancy aids (personal flotation devices) that give the torso all-round impact protection. Although there are rules against dangerous play, quite a high level of

Polo flotation aids have additional padding in the sides to protect the torso against injuries caused by heavy impact from other boats and paddles.

A polo player about to shoot for a goal. He has simply dropped his paddle across the deck to free both his hands.

protection is necessary. Helmets have wire face guards, and paddles have a minimum blade thickness and radius to minimize injuries that might occur with a sharp edge. Ramming and other aggressive play is not allowed, although, like ice hockey, the game is a contact sport with plenty of pushing and shoving. Since the paddles and hands can be used to control the ball and to block opponents' shots and passes, it is inevitable that there will be firm contact and clashes of boats, paddles and heads. It is quite common to be pushed in by an opposing player while trying to play the ball, although there are strict rules on where on the body the player can be pushed (shoulders and arms only).

Being an explosive sport it is incredibly good exercise with plenty of sprinting, braking, accelerating, rolling and hand-rolling, as well as ball handling. Play

regularly and you will be incredibly fit. You do need to warm up and stretch before playing, though, otherwise the severe physical demands you place on your body may result in injury. The best thing about playing in an indoor pool is that it will be heated.

Although there are specialist polo boats, most clubs will have a selection of pool training boats and paddles, which are often used. If you join a local canoe club that plays polo, you will probably be able to take part without buying any gear. If you take only one piece of kit, make it a nose clip. You can only enjoy getting chlorine up your nose for so long.

For more information or the address of your local club, contact either your national governing body for paddle sport, or a local kayak or canoe store in your area that may be able to put you in touch with a relevant organization.

Dragon Boat Racing

The phenomenally popular sport of dragon boat racing dates back to early China. With boats powered by up to 20 paddlers they charge through the water, and make a fantastic sight when decked out in traditional colours.

How It Developed

Dragon boat racing originated in China more than 2,000 years ago. According to legend there was a warrior-turned-poet by the name of Qu Yuan. A loyal subject of the emperor, he was overcome with sorrow at the poverty and corruption that was then rife in the country. He protested by committing suicide, throwing himself into the Mi Lo River. When his followers heard of his death, they took to the river in their boats, beating the water with their paddles, and threw rice dumplings into the river to feed his spirit.

From that time onwards, the Chinese people commemorated the death of the heroic Qu Yuan by holding the annual Dragon Festival. Since then, dragon boat racing has become a widespread sport. In fact, some sources claim it is the

◉ *Dragon boating hosted as a fun event by the British Army's Royal Marines.*

second largest participation sport in the world, after soccer. This may be due to its enormous popularity throughout China, and its more widespread use as a commercial adventure sport in other parts of the world. Anyhow, the sport of dragon boat racing only really came to the West in the early 1980s. Since then it has grown steadily, and thousands of people now take part each year.

◉ *A ladies' dragon boat team in action. Synchronized paddle strokes are vital.*

Taking Up Dragon Boating

The first step is to find a club, or go to a session run by an outdoor centre. You can find them extremely easily on an internet search engine by typing in "dragon boating" for whichever country you are in.

Paddles for dragon boating are like canoe paddles, but they are shorter because of the lower sitting position. Serious practitioners use traditional wooden paddles, but centres and club boats more usually use plastic ones. Women often use paddles that have a thinner shaft and T-grip. With a really strong crew of 20 the boat practically lifts out of the water with every stroke, and can be powered at more than 4m (13ft) per second. In a race, there is always a drummer at the front who beats in time with the stroke paddler. This is an important job because if the drum is out of time the crew will be too.

For training and individual performance comparison, dragon boat racers paddle the racing K1s with an outrigger attached for balance, and they use a dragon boat paddle. Competitions are held in most countries, with national and world championship events held regularly.

Traditionally, a dragon boat is decorated with a colourful dragon's head and tail, and has scales painted all over the sides.

⬆ *This team's optional warpaint matches the livery of their dragon boat and adds enjoyment to the ride.*

⬇ *A hard-charging dragon boat crew, with the drummer in the front and the steersman aft.*

Kayak and Ski Surf Competition

If you want to go in for kayak and ski surf competitions, you have got to learn the special rules and techniques. Incredible fun, they are well worth trying on a good beach with first-rate surf.

Competitive kayak surfing is managed by national governing bodies for kayaking in many countries, and there may also be a governing body for wave-ski paddling. There are regular local and national events in many countries, and bi-annual world championships in both of these surfing disciplines.

Scoring System

Surfing is very much a freestyle discipline, but unlike freestyle kayaking in white water, points are awarded for riding a particular part of the wave rather than for tricks performed *ad hoc*. The usual format is for a heat of four paddlers at a time going out in the surf for a set period, usually of 20 minutes. Judges on the shore will award points (typically out of a total of 20) for the length and quality of the rides of each surfer on the wave. At the end of the heat, the two highest scoring paddlers out of the four will go through to the next round.

🔽 *A short, high-performance class kayak charges a steep section of surf.*

Eventually, there will be a final heat of four paddlers, who will be scored in the same way as in the earlier rounds. Sometimes there will be a head to head, with only two paddlers going out in the water at a time, to make the competition more dramatic. This sort of drama is often added for the benefit of television.

🔼 *A 3.5m (11½ft) International Class surf kayaker in action.*

To score highly in a surf competition, you need to be good at selecting waves that will give you the best possible ride. You then need to take off in just the right place to make your position in the power pocket as perfect and dynamic as possible, and use all your skills and manoeuvres to maintain that position throughout the ride, before exiting the fading wave with a flamboyant and impeccably-controlled manoeuvre.

🔽 *Straight take-off on a wave-ski. The paddler focuses on his balance.*

What the Judges Look For

On a wave-ski, you can carry on riding the wave after it has broken and the judges will carry on increasing your score for the length of ride, and for every impressive manoeuvre you make. In a kayak surfing competition, you will lose points for riding in the broken wave, unless you regain a shoulder and revert to riding in a power pocket. This reflects the different ways in which skis and kayaks handle the breaking wave; the finned and lightweight ski is a safer craft to ride in the broken wave because it is less inclined to go sideways out of control, and is easier to move off the wave.

To enter a competition you should be a member of the national governing body for your discipline (which will often provide insurance). You will be made aware of the regulations for your craft and equipment, which includes a leash for skiers, and a flotation aid and helmet for kayakers. Kayaks must be fitted with airbags, footrests and end toggles because end loops can be very dangerous in the surf.

⊙ A women's ski competitor on a custom, composite wave-ski craft.

⊙ Driving a ski through a carving turn on a beautiful, glassy shoulder.

Safety and Rescue

While good planning and appropriate equipment can prevent many difficulties, accidents will still happen. This section is intended to tell you about the safety and rescue techniques that all kayakers and canoeists need to know, whatever type of water they are paddling on. More detailed advice, including essential equipment, aimed at specific types of paddling is given in the flat water, white water and open water sections of this book.

Practise the following techniques to a proficient level, and make sure you know how to use the equipment you have with you. In a situation where every second counts, it is vital that you know what to do.

Communication

The biggest part of safety and rescue on the water is communication. Make sure you know your paddling group's level of ability and experience, so that you will be better prepared if an incident occurs. If you come across a situation involving people you don't know, start a dialogue immediately. You can't bring your skills to bear on the situation until you have understood what is happening.

● *Attempting a chase boat rescue to help a swimmer out of the water.*

Rescue and Recovery

If someone in your group is unable to re-enter their boat after a capsize, you may have to rescue them by paddling over and helping them to get back in. If they are unable to paddle due to injury or tiredness, you may need to tow them and their boat back to safety.

The following rescue and recovery techniques detail how to do this. Learn them all so that you can use the most appropriate for the situation on the day.

● *Talking through the plans for the trip in advance can eliminate confusion later.*

Chase Boat Rescue

If a paddler is in the water and unable to re-enter their boat, you may be able to get them to hold the front or back of your boat, or even get on to or into your boat, so that you can carry them to shore. It is slow progress, and often better to get to shore and use a throw-line to pull them in.

When you attempt to rescue someone who is upset or panicking, they may be irrational and can unwittingly put you in danger by clinging to you or clambering on to your boat. Don't let a victim get hold of you until you have established verbal and eye contact, and you are sure they are not going to put both of you in more danger than you are already in.

SAFETY RULES
• Always wear a flotation aid, and put it on before you get into the boat.
• Learn how to capsize as a priority.
• It is more important to rescue the victim than the boat.
• Never undertake a rescue that puts you or the victim in more danger than you were already in.
• Only ever practise rescue procedures in a safe environment.

⬆ *A shoulder belay is one way to pull a swimmer or boat from the water.*

Throw-line

A throw-line consists of a length of rope that will float tied to a bag. The bag will often have some foam buoyancy to keep it afloat as well. In order to rescue a swimmer when you are standing on the bank, take the throw-line, open the bag and grasp the loose end of the rope, and throw the bag to the victim. Aim to land the bag beyond the swimmer, so that the rope falls across him, and he can grab it and be pulled to safety.

Shoulder Belay

This is an efficient way to maximize your strength when using a rope to rescue a paddler or equipment from the bank against a fairly strong current. Wrap the rope around your back and over your shoulder to get your whole weight behind the pull. This way you can apply a force to the rope equal to about 110 per cent of your body weight. Pulling with your arms will only give you about 80 per cent.

Pulleys for Mechanical Advantage

If you are trying to recover a swimmer or a boat against a current that is too strong to resist manually, you can set up a pulley system from the bank to increase the strength of your pull.

Karabiners can be used with a sling to make a pulley. Karabiners are strong metal devices used for connecting ropes and slings to each other, or to boats and rescue equipment. They can also be used as improvised pulleys. You can attach a karabiner to a tree or rock with a sling, then put a throw-line through it to apply some braking to a swamped boat as it hurtles downstream. A boat full of water is a heavy projectile and you will not be able to control it otherwise. Karabiners are not as good as real pulleys because they apply a lot of friction, but this can be used to your advantage if you need to brake or control a descent or rescue.

If you use a pulley to double the force you apply to the boat, you will have to pull 2m (6½ft) of rope through the system for every 1m (3½ft) that the boat moves. With two pulleys, in a system called a Z-drag, there will be three times more force, but you will need even more rope. You also need to ask yourself whether you want to carry hardware such as pulleys every time you go on the river, and whether it might not be safer to abandon the boat and concentrate on rescuing only the swimmer.

Towing

A waist tow is a useful technique to operate from your boat. It can be used for towing a boat or a swimmer. It can also be used by two or more paddlers in a yoked or husky tow, which is invaluable for towing over long distances or in difficult conditions.

Using a proper towline, which will have a shock absorber to prevent spinal injury, loop the towline over your shoulder so that it can be quickly released if you become entangled with something in the water, or if you capsize, which would put you and the victim in further difficulties.

A simple 2m (6½ft) sling can be used in place of a towline for towing a boat or paddle. Put the sling around your elbow or shoulder. Never put it around your waist or body: you must be able to get rid of it easily if you capsize, even if the tow is keeping it under tension.

Modern flotation aids for white water incorporate a quick-release rescue belt as part of the design. This provides a stronger attachment for the towline.

Air Sea Rescue

Helicopters are often used to rescue kayakers from the sea or from remote wilderness rivers. You are unlikely to have experienced a helicopter rescue before, and it pays to know what to expect.

Helicopters make a lot of down-draught with their rotors. If you are afloat in a boat and one hovers overhead, it is like getting a trashing in a hole or in the surf. You will be blown over, and may not be able to roll up. It has been known for sea kayaks to be blown end over end across the water by the power of a helicopter's down-draft.

If a winchman or unmanned strop is lowered to you from a helicopter, you may need to allow for the strop to be earthed to ground on water before you try to grab it. Helicopters can generate a potentially lethal amount of static electricity which must be released to earth.

If an Air Sea Rescue helicopter is called out to recover you, they will not transport your kayaks and equipment. In fact, at sea they will deliberately sink your kayak to prevent potential false call-outs when an empty boat is spotted by shipping.

⬇ *Most countries have an Air Sea Rescue service that will come to the help of paddlers in trouble at sea.*

Medical Knowledge for Paddlers

Kayaking and canoeing are very safe sports when compared to most other adventure activities, and much safer than team contact sports such as football, basketball, rugby or cricket. However, minor injuries are commonplace in all sports, and in addition to knowing how to cope with them, you must also be aware of problems that are specific to paddlers.

The skills required to tackle serious and/or life-threatening injuries in a remote environment cannot be learnt from a book. If you intend to paddle in situations where such threats are possible, it is vital that you go on a registered first-aid course to practise the techniques involved.

Of the few injuries that do occur, most happen while actually paddling, and not while capsizing, rolling or swimming.

The most common mechanism of serious injury is striking an object such as a rock, paddle or another kayak. The next most common are traumatic stress injuries caused by the impact of water against the body or equipment, and overuse injuries such as tendon problems, particularly in the wrists, and chronic back problems.

◗ *A bivvy bag can be used to retain heat and prevent wind chill. Note here the buoyancy aid being used as a pillow to stabilize the head position and maintain clear airways.*

Minor Cuts and Bruises

Cuts, bruises and splinters are far more likely than fractured limbs. Immersion of the affected area in cold water and/or wind chill ensures that minor cuts and bruises will not usually become painful until you get off the water. If there is an open wound, however small, be aware that it might get infected and decide whether to close or cover the wound before the wound gets wet, if you still have a choice. Clean water (fresh or sea), should be used to clean the wound, and this will temper any pain. If you suspect the water is dirty, keep the wound dry.

◔ *Rolling up with the head tucked on to the front deck can save you from knocks to the head and facial injuries.*

Hypothermia

If you become excessively cold you will slowly succumb to hypothermia unless you are able to warm up your body. The victim is unlikely to realize it themselves, but early symptoms may be noticed by other paddlers. These include:
• Irrational behaviour.
• Loss of co-ordination.
• Loss of communication skills.
• Memory lapse.
• Loss of motivation and will to move.

Hypothermia can be caused by sudden cooling, for example taking a swim in cold water, or by slow progressive cooling through the onset of exhaustion and/or inadequate insulation over a period of hours. The cause might even be a combination of the two. With the former, it is correct to warm up the victim quickly, when back on land, using a warm bath or shower, or switch on the car heater.

In the case of profound hypothermia caused by slow heat loss, this would be ineffective, extremely dangerous and could result in heart failure. Instead, get the victim dry and insulate them as much as possible with clothing, a hat, gloves, sleeping bag or anything else to hand. If you are carrying a bivvy bag as part of your first aid kit, you can put the victim into it. If necessary, you can get into the bivvy bag with them to increase the temperature. Check constantly that their air passage is clear, and get professional medical help as quickly as possible. The victim will not be able to do anything to help himself.

Remember that prevention is better than cure. If you or anyone in your paddling group is exhibiting the normal signs of getting cold, for example shivering, and loss of feeling in the extremities, while on the water, act immediately before hypothermia can set in. Get the person away from the water, and get them warm.

Hyperthermia

The opposite of hypothermia is heatstroke, also known as hyperthermia. The symptoms are loss of colour, a high temperature but not necessarily sweating, and shallow breathing. The victim will feel faint and nauseous. Cool down the casualty gently by moving them into the shade and giving them lots of cool fluids.

By far the most common cause of hyperthermia in paddlers is moving around off the water when it is hot, while still wearing all the insulation that was intended for the colder conditions on the water. The best immediate treatment is to remove as many levels of clothing as necessary to enable them to cool down before they overheat.

Shock

Traumatic injury or a frightening experience can lead to shock. Similar symptoms to those of hypothermia occur. The victim may be disorientated and not capable of looking after themselves. Shock can be treated as follows:
• Treat the cause if it is physical.
• Make the victim comfortable, and place them in the recovery position if possible.
• Keep the victim warm, and provide warm drinks if there is no reason to preclude this (if the victim is unconscious or has a head or facial injury).
• Watch the victim constantly in case they stop breathing or fall in the water.
• Provide professional medical attention as soon as possible.

EMERGENCY ACTION

A realistic attitude towards personal safety on the water is essential, and a few common sense precautions will ensure you are as prepared as you can be for an emergency. Attending a registered first-aid course will give you confidence in your ability to react swiftly, and can help save lives. Contact your local kayak or canoe club for details of appropriate courses in your area.
• Drowning poses an ever-present threat to paddlers of all levels and on all types of water. Knowing how to treat a drowning person can mean the difference between life and death. First aid treatment for drowning always begins with cardiopulmonary resuscitation, and while it is beyond the scope of this book to teach this, it is recommended that you attend a first-aid course to learn what to do. The threat of drowning can be minimized by following three basic rules:
  1. The ability to swim 50m (170ft) in light clothing.
  2. Personal flotation aids should be worn at all times.
  3. A minimum number of three people in any paddling group.
• Anyone who is unconscious or semi-conscious must be placed in the recovery position to ensure that their breathing remains unobstructed. Make sure your first-aid training includes the recovery position.
• If you need to telephone the rescue services for help, find out your exact location before you call so that they know where to look for you. Include an up-to-date 1:50,000 map and a compass as part of your safety equipment, as well as a torch to help you read it if the light is poor, and give accurate map co-ordinates for where you are when you make the call.
• Keep your first-aid training up to date, and practise safety and rescue procedures with your group on a regular basis. Practising in conditions where the emergency is likely to happen – such as on a river bank in wet and windy weather – is particularly useful.

Head Injuries

These can be caused by anything from low-hanging tree branches to rocks in the water when you capsize. Anyone suffering a severe blow to the head or who becomes unconscious for any reason needs professional medical advice as quickly as possible. If this happens when the group is out on the water, return the victim to the shore, and put them in the recovery position until help arrives. Do not move the victim unless it is absolutely essential.

⊙ *Improvise an effective stretcher using two kayak paddles and flotation aids.*

❯ *Warming up and stretching thoroughly before paddling is a good way to prevent injury and mishap on the water.*

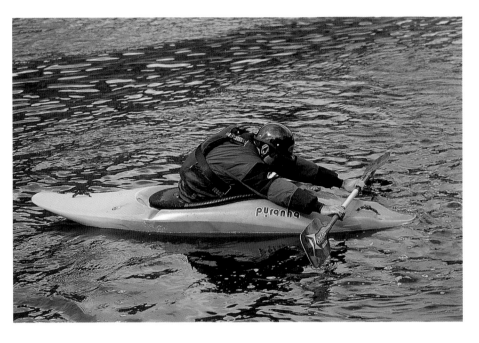

Cramp

Cramp is a painful muscle spasm that occurs when the blood supply to the affected area is impaired. It commonly affects paddlers because of their sitting or kneeling position, especially in cold weather conditions.

The condition is not serious but the pain can be severe. The best treatment is to try to stretch the muscle, counteracting its contraction, and to massage the whole area to improve the circulation. Cramp can occur in any muscle but it is particularly common for boaters to get it in the calves and the feet.

Cold Hands

Paddling in very cold water can cause extreme discomfort in the hands and particularly in the fingers. Unfortunately, the instinct to stop and warm up the hands can prolong the time you are on the water and the discomfort. A good solution is to carry on paddling and getting wet, ignoring the fact that your

❍ *A group of kayakers venturing out to sea with a qualified instructor.*

fingers are getting cold, until they really begin to hurt. If, at this point, you continue to exercise quite hard, you can provoke a reaction from your blood vessels which, though initially painful, will after a few minutes stop the discomfort. You will then be able to use your hands normally and can continue paddling.

Surfer's Ear

Surfer's ear, also known as exostoses, is an increasingly common complaint among paddlers who regularly get

completely wet. The complaint is the growth of bony lumps in the inner ear as a result of the ear canal being constantly exposed to cold water and wind chill. After a several years of regular exposure, the lumps can impair the hearing, and will cause constant ear infections by preventing the inner ear from drying out as quickly as it normally would. The best preventative measure is to protect the ears whenever you paddle by wearing a skull cap or earplugs. These are available from most paddling suppliers. Consult your doctor if you suspect you might have surfer's ear.

Shoulder Dislocation

One of the most common traumatic injuries experienced by canoeists and kayakers is shoulder dislocation, and in particular anterior dislocation (where the upper arm is forced up and back beyond its normal range of movement until the shoulder joint is dislocated). In rare cases the joint is able to relocate on its own, but more usually it will have to be repositioned by an expert medical practitioner. The injury is extremely painful, precluding further activity of any sort, and usually requiring evacuation. All you can do is to try to stabilize the injury to prevent further pain and damage. It usually takes months to rehabilitate from a dislocation, so prevention is the way to go. Avoid high bracing, reaching too far behind you, and paddling without first warming up.

FIRST AID KITS

Always carry a basic first aid kit and include the following items. Look through the equipment in your kit, and make sure you know how to use it. Better still, attend a first aid course so that you can practise the theory.

• First aid manual.
• Sterile bandages.
• Sterile plasters.
• Sterile gauze and burn patches.
• Mild relief tablets for headaches, nausea, and bacterial infection.
• Surgical tape.
• Scissors and tweezers.
• Thermometer.

Correct hand and arm position

Spine

Correct seat and leg alignment

Tendonitis

Paddlers are prone to tendon problems, particularly in the wrists and elbows. This tends to be a chronic (ongoing) complaint, which can best be addressed by using paddles with low angles of feather, and simply not overdoing it. Gripping the paddle too tightly when anxious can exacerbate the problem, as can paddling aggressively with a poor or jerky technique.

Back Pain

Back pain is common for kayakers and canoeists alike. Back problems can be minimized by good all-round training,

◯ *A dislocated shoulder or arm injury can be stabilized very effectively using a flotation aid in this manner.*

warm-up and stretching routines, but you must also concentrate on maintaining a good body posture.

The spine needs to maintain a correct curvature, with particular attention given to the curve in the lower back. A kneeling canoeist can more easily maintain this posture while paddling, while a kayaker will find it almost impossible. Failure to maintain correct lower back posture while working hard can result in severe back pain. The problem is compounded if you get into a car without adequate lumbar support to drive home. Lying in the bath at home will further aggravate the condition, as the bath floor is sloping and not flat.

◯ *An awkward capsize can easily lead to injury if there are any rocks or boulders beneath the water surface.*

◯ *Perfect posture, with the spine in the shape of a letter S, reduces pressure on the invertebral discs in the lower back.*

Perfect Posture

All back pain should first be tackled by checking the posture. Perfect posture is the position of the seated spine when there is the least amount of pressure on the intervertebral discs in the lower back. Every spine has it own unique shape. When this shape is preserved the posture is perfect. However, the human spine is a vertical flexible column that was not designed to be seated. Perfect posture is nearly impossible to attain for long periods: it must be supported. Holding the spine in the shape of a letter S when kneeling, sitting or standing will support the spine and maintain perfect posture.

Index